ZYGMUNT MOLIK'S VOICE AND BODY WORK

Zygmunt Molik is one of the last living members of Jerzy Grotowski's original acting company and was a leading trainer at the Teatr Laboratorium. *Zygmunt Molik's Voice and Body Work* explores the unique development of voice and body exercises throughout his career in actor training.

This book, constructed from conversations between Molik and author Giuliano Campo, provides a fascinating insight into the methodology of this practitioner and teacher, and focuses on his 'Body Alphabet' system for actors, allowing them to combine both voice and body in their preparatory process.

The book is accompanied by a DVD containing the films *Zygmunt Molik's Body Alphabet* (2009), *Dyrygent* (2006), which illustrate Molik's working methods, and *Acting Therapy* (1976), exploring his role in the Theatre of Participation, and also includes an extensive photo gallery documenting Zygmunt Molik's life and work.

Zygmunt Molik was a co-founder, leading actor and for 25 years a member of Jerzy Grotowski's Teatr Laboratorium. He played the main role in forming the voice training initiated by Jerzy Grotowski. His Voice and Body training sessions focus on the release of creative energy and the search for the unity and connection between the body and the voice as the basis of an actor's process.

Giuliano Campo is an actor, writer and director. He is the former Research Associate for the British Grotowski Project based at the University of Kent, UK, a member of the European Theatre Research Network (ETRN) and of the Leverhulme International Research Network collaborating with the school of the Moscow Art Theatre (MXAT).

ZYGMUNT MOLIK'S VOICE AND BODY WORK

The Legacy of Jerzy Grotowski

Giuliano Campo with Zygmunt Molik

Routledge
Taylor & Francis Group

LONDON AND NEW YORK

First published 2010
by Routledge
2 Park Square, Milton Park, Abingdon, Oxon OX14 4RN
Simultaneously published in the USA and Canada
by Routledge
270 Madison Avenue, New York, NY 10016

Routledge is an imprint of the Taylor & Francis Group, an informa business

© 2010 Giuliano Campo and Zygmunt Molik

Typeset in Times New Roman by
Bookcraft Ltd, Stroud, Gloucestershire

Printed and bound in Great Britain by
TJ International Ltd, Padstow, Cornwall

British Library Cataloguing in Publication Data
A catalogue record for this book is available from the British Library

Library of Congress Cataloging in Publication Data
A catalog record for this book has been requested

ISBN 10: 0–415–56846–3 (hbk)
ISBN 10: 0–415–56847–1 (pbk)
ISBN 10: 0–203–85186–2 (ebk)
ISBN 13: 978–0–415–56846–3 (hbk)
ISBN 13: 978–0–415–56847–0 (pbk)
ISBN 13: 978–0–203–85186–9 (ebk)

CONTENTS

ILLUSTRATIONS

Images of the 'Body Alphabet'

Photographs

*Following: pictures from all Teatr Laboratorium productions directed
by Jerzy Grotowski*

Beyond Theatre

PREFACE

This publication, instigated by Talia Rodgers of Routledge, is the result of over three years of field research conducted with Zygmunt Molik on his own work. It comes as a result of my role as research associate for the British Grotowski Project based at the University of Kent, funded by the AHRC. Nevertheless, as you will see, it has not turned out to be a typical piece of institutional research.

Polish actor Zygmunt Molik has always been my role model and hero. When I was a drama student in Rome and a young theatre practitioner I spent innumerable hours watching and analysing his astonishing stage performance in the video of the famous 1960s production of *Akropolis* by Wyspiański, directed by Jerzy Grotowski and celebrated as one of the twentieth century's theatre masterpieces.

Molik was the leading actor of Grotowski's company Teatr Laboratorium. When the company was formed, at the end of the 1950s, he was its only professional actor, older and more experienced than Grotowski himself. His early and imaginative approach to voice, as it connects to body, was developed through his role as a teacher within the company. It had a radical and transformative impact on the vocal training of actors and on theatre practices all over the world, just as the *exercises plastiques* created by Rena Mirecka (another founder and teacher of Grotowski's company) had on the physical training of actors.

While Grotowski, the 'spiritual' guide of the company, was developing his technical skills as a theatre director and theorist in collaboration with the literary advisor Ludwik Flaszen, he worked alongside Molik on the development of this innovative approach to voice, which is still highly influential in contemporary theatre.

During this period the practice of laboratory theatre, which was originated by Stanislavski, was revolutionised. From then on laboratory work could no longer be conceived purely in terms of technical achievements and skills directed towards the creation of performances for the audience's entertainment. Instead, it became a privileged setting for 'the work on oneself' that was soon open to participants from outside the company, with a variety of backgrounds and motivations, to experience.

When I first approached Zygmunt Molik with the task of documenting his work, I was ready to contribute to the canon of apologetic biographical literature. Bookshops abound with these kinds of texts, where the names of the editors are hidden behind the name of the artist being celebrated, and are padded as research, or merely as handbooks. But that was not possible: Molik did not want to talk about himself.

While following him closely and studying his art and personality, I soon realised that Zygmunt did not like to give an explanation of his work in public, and that was why his ideas on actor training had never been published in full form. Even during the practical sessions, his favourite way of working was always to use a kind of dense silence. That is, giving a few key words to begin with, followed by long pauses. You can understand it or not. If you do not, never mind. Work and you will. It succeeds marvellously when you are in his presence, and my duty was to try to find a way of making his process function in the written form. In order to do this I had to, and in all honesty I was honoured to, become his student, his pupil and companion in a practical and intellectual adventure. Now I am aware, even more than before, that the theatre and the understanding of it are not, cannot and should not be easy.

Finally the text (with the accompanying DVD on Molik's method, called 'Body Alphabet'), based on conversations and practical sessions, has been edited as a series of nine meetings, illustrating a process of transmission of experience that is core to Molik's approach in the theatre and beyond it. The focus shifted, and the new, inner obligation that I had to attend to was making this process clear; however, I was aware that I had to negotiate this within the strict demands of the scientific community.

Still, the beginning of this story is older than the project and I find it worthwhile to use a few words here talking about the unusual circumstances that brought about this rare collaboration. In fact, the first time I had a chance to meet closely with Zygmunt Molik had been a few years earlier, when I delivered a set of French cheeses to him. I was given this task by one of his students from Switzerland, with whom I was sharing a hostel during the 2005 session of ISTA (the International School of Theatre Anthropology directed by Eugenio Barba).

The ISTA sessions are itinerant and irregular, this one took place in the elegantly old-fashioned watery town of Wrocław, Poland, and was organised in collaboration with the Grotowski Institute, which is based there. The Institute is now devoted to preserving the memory of Jerzy Grotowski and his Teatr Laboratorium, as well as to the task of continuing his views and working principles. Grotowski lived in Italy for many years, where he died in 1999, however most of his work was carried out in Wrocław, and this is where Molik, who worked with his company for its entire existence, still lives.

This particular ISTA session took place at a very special time, because while the theatre sessions were running (involving teachers, artists and participants from all over the world), in Rome the Polish Pope died and suddenly around us the population of Wrocław started to mourn in such a moving way that it is hard to describe without sounding rhetorical. A huge wave of emotion was already in the air, and this confusing whirlwind of feelings came with me when this adventure in theatre began.

So to continue, this student of Molik's had to leave the ISTA session early and she put into my hands the cheeses that she had brought for Molik and had jealously protected from the daily attacks of hungry drama students. And so I met him.

Before then I knew only about the mythology of the man; the protagonist of *Akropolis* (the litany that he sings toward the end of it still resonated inside me during that, my first visit to Poland) or the creator of these strange and mysterious physical and vocal techniques such as the 'resonators' that in theatrical circles are considered almost mystical.

Of course at that time I used to try to practise some of these techniques (now, I would say just some vague ideas of them) with my theatre groups in Rome, just like thousands of other practitioners all over the planet in search of Grotowski's 'holy actor'. This is just one of many inspiring formulations of which his cult book *Towards a Poor Theatre* has plenty.

Yet, I met the man, and the myth stepped to the back of my mind, needless to say, without vanishing completely. As we got to know each other through conceiving this project, Zygmunt and I formed a friendship that was enriched on the many occasions that we enjoyed sharing good food and wine together; I would not dare to visit him and his lovely wife Eva without a bottle of their favourite Pomerol.

Whilst having such a great time with him, I was continually given insight into his essential experience and my knowledge in the theatre and beyond it significantly evolved. Working on this book gave me the opportunity to make this progress effective and to share it coherently in my own practice and teaching.

Again, what was initially intended to be made to give information about Molik's life and vision of the theatre, and about his past and present techniques (students, researchers will find lot of useful and original material in it) developed as the written result of a process of direct inner communication initiated with Molik several years ago. The text does not provide a report of the practical training and theatrical work that occurred during my time with Molik. This is because from the beginning it was clear that, due to Molik's specific approach, the final form of this document should not be a practical manual. I have taken great care to remove anything that might confuse a reader who would be looking to be told what to do.

Like the book, the accompanying videos are just traces that illustrate his work through shadows and signs that the studious observer must use in a personal way, rather than taking them as guides for the practitioner. Nevertheless, parts of both do give specific insights into the work, and the whole fifth chapter is devoted to the 'Body Alphabet' and accompanied by a full gallery of stills taken from the video. This video was made by me, with the technical support of Heather Green and with very few financial and technical means, in Portuguese actor Jorge Parente's flat of a few square metres in a *banlieue* of Paris. It was shot in a few hours while there was still some daylight left, edited during a night in a cheap hotel room at the Bastille, and shown and completed the day after at Molik's apartment in order to capture Zygmunt's relevant comments. There was deliberately no aesthetic aim in the making of the film, to avoid giving any impression of providing a flashy 'exercise video'. It was made exclusively to record and illustrate the principal actions created by Molik that no one, until now, had ever managed to document correctly.

Not all of the 'letters' of the 'Body Alphabet' are shown in the DVD; there are a few more that we decided not to include, because it must be made clear that this is not a recipe for the student to follow without creative involvement. We could not risk being misunderstood and thought to be supplying a 'method' with a step-by-step guide to acting. The DVD provides video footage of most of the actions from the 'Body Alphabet' for the purpose of clarifying Molik's work.

Right at the beginning of the book you will see indeed that Molik's explication of the nature of his work is as 'shamanic'. To a modern reader it may be difficult to accept such a perspective; however, the whole text must be read in this light. The film *Dyrygent* (made in 2006) is included because it shows Molik at work with the group in the historic site of Brzezinka in the surroundings of Wrocław; although it doesn't give an explanation of the technical process, it does in fact complement the film of the 'Body Alphabet'. As does the third film, *Acting Therapy* (1976), also never released before. This includes fragments of sessions led by other members of Teatr Laboratorium, such as Antoni Jahołkowski, Stanisław Ścierski and Rena Mirecka at work on her 'plastic exercises'. This is the only film ever made at that time on what is called 'Paratheatre' and it cross-references directly to the text.

I hope that an attentive confrontation between the three films and the book will provide an acceptable, limited though reasoned picture of Molik's Voice and Body work, both with individuals and with groups.

The Voice and Body work, using this specific name, was initiated in the mid-1970s, the time that is known as Grotowski's 'Paratheatre' or 'Theatre of Participation' phase, which followed the period of 'Theatre of Productions' (readers can refer to the appendix for a more detailed description of the phases of Grotowski's work). Voice and Body includes the 'Body Alphabet', which Molik conceived as an evolution of the principles of the work that he used as actor and leader of Grotowski's company during the 'Theatre of Productions'. Changing its focus and aims, he developed it as a tool for the work on the self, alongside its pragmatic use in actor training, so even after the dissolution of the company in 1984 it was used by Molik during his work sessions. The Voice and Body work then allowed Molik to meet and teach thousands of practitioners all over the world for more than thirty years.

During the process of creating this publication I was very often pushed to recall the many precious insights that I had received during the course of my previous training. I was lucky enough to be taught that there are two kinds of books in the theatre: one kind contains and reports facts or experiences; the other kind constitutes an experience in itself, which the author aims to transmit in order to make it endure and continue through the readers' own work. These we call 'theatres in form of books'. Our text, as a result of a close collaboration and a tight link between the two authors, has ultimately been conceived with such 'organic' intention.

Indeed after we started working together, I became progressively aware that Zygmunt had a stronger influence on me as a human being, rather than as an artist and researcher. The choice of a life in theatre can be casual and might become professional, turning to craft, but sooner or later it always comes to reveal itself as a discipline that orientates one's behaviour and way of thinking, a particular way to approach and view reality. I reached the conclusion that my main concern should be to illustrate the dialogue between us and the process of learning and transmitting skills instead of simply providing a solitary monologue. My wish is for the text to be approached as a living body and that the reader be able to experience it from my perspective.

I am aware that the importance of the text lies exclusively in Zygmunt's words; nevertheless, we believed that excluding my interventions could easily result in a flat and contrived style. This contributes to making the book alive and to vividly rendering Molik's real personality to the reader. That is why the language is not and cannot be academic, and at the same time it is not exactly informal.

The reader who is intimately interested in grasping the secret of Molik's work is accompanied by my presence in the text. In this kind of maieutic dialogue the reader has been offered all the necessary tools to enable him or her to take my place as Molik's counterpart, with all the obstacles that are involved in such an approach.

I feel the need to advise the reader that this text reflects its own development, which, through utilising this type of dialogue, generated a mutual and free exchange, and besides this it shows two non-natives communicating in English in a private environment. The text may not be considered to be balanced and structured as a 'good' scholarly and critical publication should be. Nevertheless, the primary investigative approach of a historian and theorist has been maintained and is present throughout. I am able to observe it from within and its architecture seems to me to be partially old and partially newly built or refurbished in different phases, where signs of the effect of time and changes of the weather have been left on the brickwork.

In case the reader wonders how, after years of research and work, editing and rethinking, the result appears so poor and scarcely organised, I would answer that, according to the same metaphor of the building, neither the builders' effort nor their experiences during its construction, nor its texture say much about its value, which in itself, rather than high or low, may in fact be non-existent. In other words, I hope that the reader's attention will focus on what in this book is not evident; I constantly worked bearing this in mind.

ACKNOWLEDGEMENTS

This publication would not have come into existence without the inspirational teaching that I have received in different times, places, forms and degrees of intensity by Franco Ruffini, Nando Taviani, Eugenio Barba and Rena Mirecka.

We received invaluable support from Eva Molik, Stefania Gardecka, Bruno Chojak and all the staff of the Grotowski Institute of Wrocław, who also provided some of the precious photographs included in the DVD.

I warmly thank Francesco Galli for his commitment and his portraits, and Maurizio Buscarino for permission to publish a piece of his masterly photographic work of Molik in rehearsal for *Apocalypsis cum figuris*.

The DVD *Zygmunt Molik's 'Body Alphabet'* resulted from the voluntary and excellent participation of Heather Green and Jorge Parente.

The text has improved significantly as a result of the gracious interventions of Jonathan Grieve and Emily Ayres. Magda Stam helped with translation of the Polish spellings.

The whole project has been constantly supported at all stages by my former research director and old friend Paul Allain, and by the enthusiasm of my editor, Talia Rodgers. Thank you all.

Giuliano Campo, September 2009

DVD ACKNOWLEDGEMENTS

DVD features the film 'Dyrygent' © Tomasz Mielnik, used by permission. 'Dyrygent' features excerpts from Karlheinz Stockhausen – Zyklus © Copyright 1960 by Universal Edition (London) Ltd., London/UE 13186. The composition in its entirety can be ordered on CD 6 of the Stockhausen Complete Edition from stockhausen-verlag@stockhausen.org. Information about Stockhausen and his music may be found at www.stockhausen.org.

DVD produced by Peter Hulton at Arts Archives – www.arts-archives.org.

1

FIRST DAY

Acting Therapy – The Voice and the Life – The beginnings

Campo: *I'd like to start our conversation about your work and your life by discussing an episode which I find exemplary. It concerns the film* Acting Therapy. *It is a rare film, shot in Wrocław, Poland, in the studio space of the Teatr Laboratorium, the company you co-founded, directed by Jerzy Grotowski. It shows the activity of a workshop you and the actor Rena Mirecka led in the mid-seventies. It clearly demonstrates the quality of your work with the participants, your ability to open the participants' voices through a personal relationship. I wonder what happened on that specific occasion, because it is visible that something extraordinary happened when you were working with that boy.*

Molik: It is a strange beginning for a book, and I like it. I agree, it is a key moment, but everything is visible there, so what can I explain? It happened in that way because I didn't know what to do. I did everything that was necessary in order to achieve my goal. My aim was that I wanted to open his voice because I knew that he had it, but he couldn't demonstrate it, simply that. So I did everything that was necessary, and that was all, and I can't say now what I did, what I was doing. I did many strange things, because I tried from one side, from another side, and so on and so on and so on … until I had it. There you can see how difficult it is. But I knew what I was doing, and in fact I reached the goal.

Campo: *At first you worked with your own voice because he didn't have any voice, and at the end he found his voice. So, what is the relationship between voice and the rest of life, why the work with the voice, and what is the voice?*

Molik: I don't know, but I got it. Now, when I think of what I did, I can tell my work was like a shaman's work. I worked like

1

a shaman, trying to make the impossible possible. It looked like nothing could be done, because he was full of so much resistance in himself, not to be opened, not to let himself be opened, and so on and so on. So I tried many things, it took such a long time. Usually I never work for so long with one 'patient' (here I can use this term), but this time I was very stubborn and finally we got it, yes.

Campo: *When you work with other students, or actors or practitioners, do you use the same approach to open energetic channels, liberating them and trying to find something, to make something hidden appear, like you did in this case?*

Molik: No, I can never do the same, because everybody is quite different. So I never engage with different challenges in the same way. My method is to find out what is the right way to truly approach someone, and this is the only way to get results. There is no such thing as a method that I can use all the time and achieve the intended result. I must guess, I must seek, I must search a lot, and then I get it. It usually takes much less time, but this case you see in the film was a very difficult one, let me say, and that is why it took such a long time. Normally, if I try to open someone's voice, then I do it in two or three minutes. It's enough. I just try different positions, on the wall or on the floor, and it's very often enough, but that time this wasn't possible. Nothing could work, so I made a kind of quest, into the absolute unknown. It was a case I have never met in my life. Because I knew that he had full voice, but he couldn't open it. Years later I had another similar case, where it didn't look possible to open someone's voice. It was near Bordeaux, Las Téoulères, a studio space in a farm. It wasn't possible to get the voice out of someone, but finally I did it after many attempts, trying this way, that way, and so on. Finally I did it very simply, I made him run, then fall down, and then cry out.

Campo: *Cry out was an instruction that you gave?*

Molik: Yes, I just said to him: 'Cry out now!' And he did, and then later, once opened, it was easy. Once I had opened the voice (later on, because it was gradual) he could keep this voice. I repeated it and told him: 'Cry out, take a breath and cry out, keep on shouting.' And he did it, and then I just regulated it, I put it into a normal channel and he started singing with his full voice.

Campo: *That's something he could never do before. It was the first time for him.*

Molik: Yes, he couldn't, before he could only blab something like 'da-da-dara-dara-ta-tari-ta-tara' with a very weak voice and he could not give a normal voice. First he opened his voice with this shouting, when he fell down and just reacted on this 'Ah!' with the whole mouth open. Then I prolonged it slowly and tried with two or three breaths, and it then became normal singing. It was then just a question of regulating this energy and this opening, to keep the energy and opening at the same time.

Campo: *I see that you worked through producing shocks in him, a physical shock, this falling down, and an emotional shock, the crying out. Do you think it is possible to work directly on emotions, to lead emotions, someone's emotions?*

Molik: No, by emotions nothing was possible. It had to be as it appeared, as it appeared to me, it must be a physical shock, no emotions. I didn't try that way because I saw his voice was physically blocked in the throat, since he produced a sound like 'aargh'.

Campo: *The crying out came as a consequence of the falling?*

Molik: It was like accumulating energy and then exploding. He did it rapidly when he heard me say 'Cry out!' It was a simple, unconscious reaction, and then he could do it consciously, but first it had to be unconscious. Just as if I had a piece of metal which stayed in the fire, and when touching him with it, he would cry out, but since I didn't use such a thing, I made him run and then fall down.

Campo: *This makes it clear that there is a deep connection between the physical shaking, the physical shocks and the voice, that stressing the body physically opens the channels to liberating the voice. I have always thought that even if the use of the voice is part of the physiology of the body, it is also evident that voice is also a link to something other than the body, and that is why working with voice can be so powerful. So, in this case you were working with voice through the body, in order to open something in a wider sense. It is an opening of the self. So there is something that opens which is not purely physical. What is opened, precisely?*

Molik: The larynx is opened.

Campo: *So it is something always and exclusively physical.*

Molik: In the end, yes, but just in the end. Anyway, the difference between the first case and the second case that I just told you about was that for the first boy I took almost a half an hour –

of which fourteen minutes are visible in the film – and for the second boy I just decided what to do after three minutes of trying this way and that way, and I made him experiment with this running and falling down, and then telling him 'Shout'.

Campo: *What happens when you work on voice with someone who is already open? What happens, what is the effect of working with the voice? Have you seen many differences between your approach to someone who is very experienced and professional or an amateur or someone coming from a very different experience, who never had any experience in theatre? Must they be approached in very different ways, or is it always a very personal relationship?*

Molik: It is very different but I don't make any distinction between amateurs and professionals, because I am working on the organism. On the whole organism. And in the first phase I leave behind anything that is connected to their experience. I mean, when I start working with the voice itself, I make no distinction between an amateur and a professional. It's the same, the organism is the same. Later on we do professional work. Monologues and songs. But the first two days everybody does the same. Only singing together. And if there is a problem with someone who has no voice, because he can't be opened, I must do that individual work, but only with these people. When I see that someone isn't able to sing at all, and can just express this sound 'agh' stuck in the throat with a low voice, then I move on and do individual work.

Campo: *The organism is the same for everybody, yes, but still, your experience comes from theatre, so how is art involved in this process? Your life was, is, a life in art, your techniques, your approach, come from art.*

Molik: Concerning those, we have to talk about something else. Until now we've been talking about the voice itself, but now I'll tell you some more and quite different things. First of all, we must find the Life. Then, only into this Life can you try to put, if it is possible to say this, the open voice. Then, from this open voice, we must move from the simple vocalisation to something like a song. Then you put the text. So this is the way I work, and for that reason I always start from a physical practice. Then, if the body is already open, and very gently at first, I try to start working on the voice, first only singing together, then listening carefully and fixing the harmony. This is so as to not have chaotic singing, but to try to find, together, a choir, a chorus, that just sounds good.

I often hear someone just shouting something like 'Uah! Uah! Uah!' and that's not what I'm looking for. He has to make a good contribution to singing together. Like a chorus. This different energy is sometimes very like singing, sometimes it's full singing with everything fully open, but for the first two days the point is just to work on the breath, on the respiration. Afterwards they can go more into the unknown, when the Life has been found. Everybody finds the Life in the self. The Life is something connected with everyone's life, his memories, or even his dreams. This is what I call 'the Life'. It's difficult to explain. The Life, when it's found, has its physical and vocal shape. Then it's not magma any longer. When we are singing together we have just the material, a kind of raw matter, materialising in this common area. After a few days, two or three days, everybody starts to go on an individual quest. Into the unknown. I'm not going to explain what the unknown means, but such a thing exists, yes, and so it is possible to find it. Someone finds it on the first day (I mean on the third day, because that is the first day of seeking, of this kind of research), someone finds it on the third day, and of course someone else at the last moment, on the fifth or the sixth day. In this kind of singing the unknown now materialises in the self, in the physical shape, in the body, and also in the voice, because the voice is a vehicle. It brings the Life up from the world. The Life itself.

Campo: *Is this something that could be related to what Grotowski used to call 'the Process', or is it totally different?*

Molik: No, it's not the same. 'The Process' comes later. The first thing must be quite simply to do this physical work in order to fully open the voice. I don't know how the larynx works technically, but it has a strong connection with the energy, also with the psyche, because the voice has different colours. All these elements must be ready. If they are not ready, because maybe at first the best way has not been found, they must at least be prepared. Everything must be already prepared in order to function together. And then we can get busy with 'the Process'. That's the basic work that must be done.

Campo: *So the voice is an instrument for connecting body and psyche.*

Molik: Yes, exactly, everything. Even the soul.

Campo: *And what is the role of the intelligence, or as you better described it, of the consciousness, since this process is both conscious and unconscious?*

Molik: The intelligence is something marginal.

Campo: *But in the end, what or who is leading the process? I was thinking of Stanislavski. For him there's a part in the performer's self that has to be aware of what's going on.*

Molik: This is the master. Intelligence is the master which is so much above the whole organism that we don't need to do any work on it.

Campo: *So, during the work sessions after this preparatory vocal moment is done, each participant has to realise something, a sort of 'partitura', a physical score. Something that is precise. What is the role of precision within this 'floating' Life?*

Molik: First of all the Life must be found. Then it must be re-found several times, and the second, the third time, the necessary corrections must be made, because certain corrections are always necessary. After that we now have the 'partitura'.

Campo: *And each participant has to repeat it. So the more you repeat, the more it becomes precise, that's how it works.*

Molik: Yes, but you don't need to repeat it too much. Repeating it two or three times is enough. Later the matter is not to lose the Life, because it is very easy to lose. When the Life inside the construction is gone, then the remaining 'partitura' is just an empty space. It's an empty construction. Then it can happen that, actually it always happens, that when you do it and when you get it the first time it's full. The second time, maybe it's still full – alive – but is too much or too little. For that reason it's necessary to construct it the second time, because it's necessary to make some corrections; very often they are very tiny. Sometimes, the second time everything is lost, and then you must go on the quest for the source of this Life. How was it found the first time? This is very interesting because it often happens that something is quite forgotten, and sometimes very much is forgotten. How to get to the source of all that? That's the most important thing. The precision.

Campo: *Is there just one source for all cases? For example, what if there's Life in one section and this is lost in another section? How do you revive this Life?*

Molik: That's the reason why the eyes are necessary. An outside eye. Very often it's not possible for someone working alone to remind himself what he did. There must be someone who has seen it the first time, when it was full, when it was good, when it was alright. Someone who would remind him about that moment and how he did it and that he did it like that and like this and like that, and then, step by step, it's possible to get to the first value of this Life.

Campo: *So there is the possibility of working from externals, and through repeating some elements, some visible details, this can help to reveal the Life.*

Molik: Exactly like that, and as a matter of fact the chances are almost fifty–fifty for someone to return to the first version without any fault. Sometimes it happens, when there is a short Life. But with a longer Life it's not possible. Practically never. There must be some corrections. Normally.

Campo: *So in that case this external eye acknowledges more than the performer himself does, since it's likely that the performer doesn't feel what's seen. So there is something objective there, that no longer stays subjective.*

Molik: Absolutely.

Campo: *I've read your article 'How the tradition passes from one to another', which is one of the few things I could find about Jury Zavatzky – Stanislavski's and Vakhtangov's follower whom Grotowski called his father after his apprenticeship at GITIS in Moscow.[1] It also explains what Grotowski got from the teachings of Stanislavski and the differences between the two approaches. Reading what you said about ethics in relation to Stanislavski and Grotowski, what came into my mind is that this is probably the main link between the two, much beyond the techniques. Concerning this issue I can say that lots of misunderstandings still exist, especially in the English-speaking world, about both Stanislavski and Grotowski, and therefore about your own work. These misunderstandings result in a sort of recipe supposedly coming from those masters, a sort of list of techniques for performing, and they completely lose the real meaning of this work, which is essentially work on the self. For instance, the English translation of the main Stanislavski book is titled* An Actor's Work,[2] *missing the importance of the original Russian, which is* The Actor's Work on the Self. *But I ask you now, where is the value in all the work with the participants that you were just talking about? Where is the ethic in this work? How would a practitioner or a student or someone working with you change? Does he change his approach to life? This is something that theoretically can change the approach to life, or it can just be a temporary work with temporary consequences. Have you seen any real change in the people working with you?*

7

Molik: Of course I see that. But I don't deal with ethics just as I don't deal with soul. Because my work is called 'Voice and Body', and ethics is rather connected with the soul. For them, for the students, for the pupils, whatever we call them, it is possible that this work involves ethics, but I don't know. I don't deal with it, unfortunately. I assume that our ethics, when we start our work, are very high and don't need any improvement. Very often I'm wrong. But I can't intervene in someone's ethics consciously. Unconsciously, probably I do.

Campo: *I would like to know how you built your role in* Akropolis.

Molik: I know that you want to know it because it was very demanding on the vocal level. It's a very demanding role. You have seen the film *Akropolis*,[3] so you noticed I performed difficult things with my voice.

Campo: *I spent many years experimenting on myself and with the people who worked with me on the kind of work you were doing at that time. I always wondered what exactly are these 'resonators'.*

Molik: Well, I can say something, but I forgot about the resonators a long time ago. It was a long time ago. When I started exploring and teaching 'Voice and Body' I started with resonators, but after a while I found it completely useless and even damaging, because the participants' attention went in the wrong direction. They started to play with resonators and vocalising, for example, a kind of 'Ahh' coming from the frontal area, just below the neck, and 'Houu' from the back of the neck, and 'Hii' from the area higher up on the back of the neck. But no, this isn't what I was looking for. Then I concentrated on the organic voice only, on how to get the organic voice from the base of the spine, how to start the resonators from the end of the vertebral column, the lowest point of the vertebral column. Later, through the singing, [I concentrated] on how to open the larynx and find the way to open the chest or the shoulders. These last years, very gently, I've tried to come back to it, but it was a very, very delicate process, because it is rather better if the search into the unknown finds the right resonator, instead of consciously using these resonators in the belly, or that resonator on the neck, etc. These last years I've tried very gently to remind people of such things like resonators, but it must be done gently; as I said, it's a very delicate matter. So I prefer not to use resonators during the work, but I try to explain them using different elements, in a quite different manner.

8

Campo: *Who was the creator of this system of exercises?*

Molik: Life. In other words, myself. I can't say what my inspiration was because nothing came from outside. It came quite simply by learning and experimenting. I started because I was interested in this kind of research, on voice. But I knew almost nothing. I just had the will to do so, and the field interested me. I got some of my knowledge step by step, but I don't know where from, because it wasn't possible to get anything from a book, from any book. When I read some books on voice, they made me laugh. I might say, always. It's not possible to say, for instance: 'do this with the larynx and make a kind of "la … la … " using the teeth'. No. Voice is a complex thing, a very complex thing. The whole body must be engaged and only you can know how to distribute some different factors, how much energy, how much subtlety, how much vibration, and so on and so on.

Campo: *What about your formation?*

Molik: I had good professors in the Warsaw Academy of Theatre which at that time was called the National Higher School of Theatre. Now it's called Academy of Theatre. I can't recall what I learnt there because, unfortunately, when I found myself on the stage, on the real stage and not in the school, it was different. In fact in the last year we did some performances, we were already performing before leaving the school, but it was in different circumstances, not on stage but in the big lecture room of our school. So when I found myself on the stage I had lots of problems with talking, with speaking. I didn't know why, since I was a very good student, I might say. I must praise myself because I always achieved the highest marks and so I got the best scholarships; I was like a lord in my time. It happened because of lack of breath. The only lessons on voice we had were just a sentence repeated on a scale, from the lowest to the highest note. So, nothing for the breath. Absolutely. Then, after that I could only speak for as long as I could sing the sentence that we repeated during the exercise, and then I had to take the breath again, and so I had problems with just speaking. And then a colleague, a lady, a young lady, a beautiful lady, helped me, because she had some ideas on voice, because her mother was a singer, a teacher of singing. And so she had some ideas and she took me aside and in a few minutes she explained to me how to breathe. After that I had no more classes on voice. But that was a good

9

lesson for me. And it made me interested in this argument, the voice, and then, when we started our theatre with Grotowski I was already a kind of expert for the others, yes. I started working on voice with everybody. Yes, that's the truth.

Campo: *You were all very young.*

Molik: Yes, yes. They needed some lessons. Not so much lessons, actually, but to do some work on voice, yes. So for a half year I was a professor of voice for the others. With Cieślak it was very interesting, because he couldn't do anything; his larynx was completely closed. And this is visible in a film.[4] He gives this 'Ahh' with a very low tone, totally blocked. Just like that, 'Ahh'. And my first work was on him. It was simple; I just made him lie on the floor, and made him lift the middle part of the body higher, balancing on the feet and on the head. In that way you must organically have the open larynx. And just in such way I made him change, because he had this bad habit of speaking that he used with everything, and always with a closed larynx. When he tried to say something officially, not privately, he gave this 'Ah', with no voice. Afterwards no, it was enough. After one week he was all right.

Campo: *One week.*

Molik: One week, yes. Maybe ten days. But he was tough, from the very beginning. He did it for one hour, the whole hour, like this 'Ahhh … Ahhh … ' and so on and so on, to open himself. But maybe I should not betray secrets. But no, these are normal things.

2

SECOND DAY

Techniques – 'Sing your Life' – Teachers
and masters – Grotowski and the
company

Campo: *I would like to know something about the technique of reaching*
        physical tiredness, using 'fatigue'[1] in order to achieve the
        results that you want, and if there is a specific way of working
        with it as a way for liberating the impulses.

Molik: Yes, 'la fatigue', when you are very tired. That's not my
        method, but it was the method of Grotowski. Yes, sometimes
        he took us to the absolutely exhausted stage.

Campo: *You spent a big part of your life working with Grotowski. I*
        wonder if you want to say something about it, or how this
        work affected your own life and work.

Molik: No. Not particularly. I would prefer not to.

Campo: *What about the work that you have done, I mean as a group,*
        with yoga?

Molik: Nothing. No, we didn't exercise with yoga. I used only a small
        physical part of it, only the Viper, which I later put into my
        'Body Alphabet'. Do you know what the Viper is?

Campo: *Do you mean the energy of Kundalini, which supposedly*
        inhabits the base of the spine?

Molik: No, I mean the snake, the position. It's the only thing I use
        from yoga.

Campo: *What about the plastic exercises, also known as 'plastiques'?*

Molik: I use these exercises a lot. In particular a part of my 'Body
        Alphabet' is based on the plastic exercises.

Campo: *But have you not created these kinds of forms?*

Molik: No, not really, because some of them were taken from this guy
        who first practised them, like turning the arms and so on.

Campo: *Some were taken from the rhythmical exercises of Dalcroze,*
        and also, I guess, from Delsarte's studies on the tripartite
        body of the human being.

Molik: Yes some of them are certainly in my 'Body Alphabet'.

Campo: *Grotowski talked also about something taken from Charles Dullin. When I think of Dullin I think of his extraordinary ability to create a good sense of the ensemble, of the group. Your work in the group was very peculiar. It wasn't like any professional, institutional, normal way of working, I mean 'normal' in the sense of what institutions want and ask from professionals. You built this company in which all the members were working together all of the time, and so created something very stable, some very stable relationships. Do you think that working with the others, and not just with a director or a single partner, but with a whole stable ensemble does affect the way of working itself?*

Molik: To tell the truth, I can't say. I don't have any answer to this, because it seems quite natural to me after so many years of work in an ensemble.

Campo: *About professional acting now: how much is it about the imitation of what a master or a teacher shows, and how much is it about invention? What would be an ideal balance of these different approaches? When is the right moment for a very strong individuality? Or when we repeat a form, an external form made by someone else, how can this be creative at the same time? How do you feel as a master when you have pupils follow you?*

Molik: I tell you what I do with the pupils, just to be concrete. I allow great freedom to everybody, because people are different; someone is already trained, someone else is very fresh. So I allow everybody freedom, someone can do exactly what I propose, and someone else approaches the exercises just slightly. And I accept this too. Both ways can be good for creativity, it depends on the people and their experiences.

Campo: *In most of the Far Eastern forms, for example, they have a vocabulary of actions which is already established and a good actor is the one who can repeat them in the most perfect way. However, you can't say they are not creative, because they find freedom inside the forms, through following and imitating them. Of course your experience was different, but I wonder if it ever happened that when someone found a form the director or you said 'yes, this is a form I want to follow' and so repeated that form. Maybe it never happened that you repeated someone else's form, and you always created the forms yourself. Obviously, in your company, in your kind of work, you had to follow the physical score, and on some occa-*

sions, like in Akropolis, *in all details. What are your general thoughts about this? This is relevant for performers like me. For instance, when I work as a commedia actor on some reinventions of commedia dell'arte this often means simply following forms which have been created by someone else, forms of the pantomime of the nineteenth and twentieth centuries. I use them because they work, but where is the creativity in it? I still wonder.*

Molik: It depends. I'll go back to the example of my work with the pupils. Sometimes I require them to repeat the actions in a very exact way, although generally speaking I don't tolerate these kinds of imitations. The fact is that the action must be full but also clean, cleanly done, but beside that I leave everybody free. If they do the actions from the 'Body Alphabet', they must be done well. The action must be done in a clean way. I always stress: 'Don't do it like a half action only.' For example, if I say 'Touch the sky', it must be really as if he enjoys touching the sky, that he wants to touch the sky, moving the arms fully to the top, not just doing 'puf, puf', slow half-movements of the arms.

Campo: *And how do you work with the imagination?*

Molik: This is up to each one. It's very important to have imagination, because otherwise what would it be? It would be just repeating some actions. Of course, I mean using imagination in order to find the true Life with true actions, so it isn't that someone is completely free, without doing the clean, full actions. Everybody should be completely free, with imagination and with all that is necessary to stimulate a creative process, while making really clean actions.

Campo: *In your work as a professional actor, I guess you've dealt more with personal memories, rather than with imagination.*

Molik: That's a quite different thing, because if one is exploring his life (I don't call this imagination), he must forget about all actions. When he goes into this imaginary life he must be just like a real person. This imaginary life must be, from the moment he starts doing it, his real life. No more imagination, but just real life. His whole person must be in it, and then he must abandon all this thinking about any actions, they must already be in the organism. That's what makes this life more complete, not just like everybody's everyday life, but it must be done wholly, with fullness, as the singular action is done in the training. I mean that the body must already be so well trained with those actions

13

that we treat as training, that later, this training can and must be completely forgotten. The body remembers that it must be more alive than in everyday life, it must be something special, a different kind of life. The life must be there, but not as small as in the everyday life; the full life has to be there. This is the reason why this process is done.

Campo: *Following this process, something that comes from our past can be shown in a new, regenerated form.*

Molik: Yes, we can say it like this.

Campo: *You must have noticed that there are different kinds of energy. Energy is not just one; there are different levels and qualities of energy.*

Molik: Of course. Sometimes we can do very small actions, but with such energy that it results in a kind of emanation. They emanate. Even if you do small gestures like moving the hand slowly, and it can mean, it can be nothing, but if this action is done taking the energy from the feet, it takes the whole body to a special presence. It goes through the whole body from the feet. Not just 'paf' 'paf', like an empty movement.

Campo: *What is the role of rhythm in building the action? Is there a real rhythm, like Stanislavski used to say, that there is a tempo-rhythm, a good one, and only one for a specific action for a specific person?*

Molik: The rhythm in the training normally works in that way. You can work in different rhythms, and normally, if the rhythm produces a certain effect of lightness, we work very lightly but energetically. It means that the body must be very light but the action must be full, that it is precisely done but very light, the rhythm must then be rather quick. But if you slow down, the energy deals with a different kind of weight and everything must be done in a slowed-down rhythm. We do also this kind of training for preparing something, yes, that is, for example, going to the bottom of the sea. Everything is very slow, with the great resistance of the water, in the depths of the bottom of the ocean. Then everything is quite different. So it's normal, natural, that the way you move is influenced by the circumstances in which you are. And if you are, for example, in the middle of a field, full of sun, you must be light; you must do the same action, but like a butterfly. The rhythm depends on the circumstances in which you are.

Campo: *So is there a moment when you might say something, for example when a pupil has a wrong attitude, and you can see*

that the rhythm is not working? It's not just a personal inter-
pretation of the rhythm. There's something very real that you
see. There's a moment when we feel that the rhythm is right.

Molik: Of course the rhythm is one of the very deciding factors. Yes,
you can see and intervene in it.

Campo: *So sometimes you can find something that is objectively right,*
or you sense it and look for it and then eventually find it.
Thinking about this topic of the right tempo-rhythm, I was
wondering whether it connects to the inner intentions while
building a character, or even when we are imitating some
fixed forms like in the commedia dell'arte, where there are
some established ancient roles which can condense most
of humanity into a single form. Some traditional roles can
explain the nature, the character of certain human beings,
and this synthesis looks objective and inter-cultural. I'm
wondering if there's a way of coming back to a memory that's
not just our own personal memory but something that even
precedes us, that's older than ourselves, which maybe results
in what is called an archetype. Is this something that you try
to find when you work with these attempts to discover the Life
in a pattern of actions?

Molik: I think it is one of the fundamental things.

Campo: *Do you ever use a specific chant, or any specific song in order*
to reveal these archetypes? I see that this method has become
very common in the theatre now.

Molik: I don't do it. It's not through this way that I try to get the
essence.

Campo: *But do you look for some kind of vibrations in the voice?*

Molik: Sometimes, yes.

Campo: *Considering that each individual's work is always different*
from one another's, where do you find their singing and their
voice?

Molik: Very often from the echo in the room. If I say: 'Sing your
Life', he must find it. First he gives one sound and then he
hears some resonances and then he knows, he must know, he
should know, how to find the other tones from that resonance,
because there are always some. Quite simply, yes, there are
always some tones that you can hear in the space as a resonance, and then you must find them and must, with that, with
what you hear, you must go on and improvise your song.

Campo: *The space itself has something in it that you have to find.*

Molik: Yes.

Campo: *How different is it to work with people of different nation-*
alities, and also working in different places? Since we were
talking about essence, everyone has the same essence, deep
inside, I guess, but there are some differences.

Molik: I think that the differences between the individual human
organisms are not so big, so it's more or less the same in every
country. There are only individual differences. Of course there
are. I didn't work often with people of other races, probably
it could be a little different, but maybe not, anyway I have to
adapt to them. I had to adapt when I worked with a Japanese
person and an Indian, but it was only one Indian boy in a group
and one or two Japanese girls in another. I rarely worked with
black people, sometimes there was a black woman, but only
one. In these cases I had to adapt to the consistency of their
organism, and then I followed their innate voice. I didn't try to
change them, but I went along with their possibilities.

Campo: *To find their own voices.*

Molik: Yes.

Campo: *May I say that I have had a long association with Chinese people*
and I remain very impressed by my visit to China. Millions of
people there practise every day some simple forms, the Taoist
exercises for health, which really help to get a direct, energetic
physical contact with the external world. I have also myself been
practising for a long time the art of Taijiquan, which I had the
good fortune to learn directly from Li Rong Mei, a great Chinese
master. These experiences strongly influenced my own theatre
practice, although they're not immediately related to the theatre.
This ability to create a conscious, direct and organic contact
between the mind and the body, the individual and the external
world, is largely lost in the West. That's why lots of people
here are interested in experimenting with something, anything
that helps to recover this connection. All human beings in the
end have to face the same big problem: our minds want to run
quickly all the time, in any possible or impossible direction, and
our bodies, on the contrary, tend to move as little as possible.
The result is disastrous, and other cultures, especially coming
from the Far East, seem to be much more aware of it than ours.
What was your approach to texts coming from the Far East, for
example Sakuntala, *Kalidasa's classic Indian text that you put on*
the stage in 1960, or something coming from another culture?

Molik: Other cultures or other languages? Because it's not the same.
I'll give you an example of when I worked with some Dutch

people. They did some work on the great monologues from *Richard III*. I gave them this task: they had to learn by heart the great monologues from *Richard III*, and they did it. Everybody brought one monologue. They learnt them in Dutch, and in Dutch I couldn't understand anything, absolutely nothing, but the words didn't matter at that time. First I asked them to find the Life, and then to sing this Life with an open voice, and then with the same voice (which was already full of feelings of course because it was connected with their life), with this voice, I asked them to just put the words on top. They spoke the monologues, long monologues, from *Richard III*. I don't mean the first one, which is rather short, but the others which are very long. I didn't know a single word of their language. However, I worked with them, this is because the meaning of the words is nothing for me, something else is important: what Life is given, the Life the person brings out with these words. What sound, what feelings with this sound, what colour with this sound, what rhythm with this sound. The meaning of the words is the last thing; it isn't my problem. It's eventually their problem to make it understandable. Quite simply, I don't mind if I don't understand anything. I just ask the others after the first attempt, after the first try, 'Did you get the sense of the text?' Yes, OK. No? So they have to do it again, do more, and try to articulate better, to make this Life cleaner, more understandable.

Campo: *Did you use a similar process in* The Constant Prince *and* Akropolis?

Molik: In *Akropolis* it was something different, but in *The Constant Prince* it was already this, yes.

Campo: The Constant Prince *is, in a way, one long song. A sort of music, but the words are very precise and very important at the same time.*

Molik: I said that in *Akropolis* it was different because the sound in *Akropolis* was composed, as well as the physical actions and all the other elements of the performance. It was a complex total composition with music. The source of the sound wasn't immediately organic, like in *The Constant Prince*. In *Akropolis* it was all a composition, I can still sing some examples. This kind of speaking was composed, and in the last part – that was when I was sitting down with some other actors – it was just like a song, like a hymn, it was a composition that could be put in notes.

Campo: *Did all the actors create their own music, or was there some-*
           thing to follow?

Molik: Most of the actors were following something, a composi-
           tion done by a musician; a musical composition of speech.
           The rhythm was also important; something with very quick
           and loud speaking, something very slow, with pauses, 'pom/
           po-pom/poom/po-pom/poom'. In *Akropolis* all the elements,
           all the scores, physical and vocal, and all the rest were prepared
           like that, yes. Everything was composed.

Campo: *About* Akropolis, *I was impressed when I heard you saying*
           that you had to do an amazing number of rehearsals. You had
           to repeat it every day for long time, because of the demands of
           your work.

Molik: We rehearsed for only three months, but we rehearsed twice a
           day. Not all the time, but the last two weeks we did it twice a
           day.

Campo: *And how many times did you have to show the work?*

Molik: More than a hundred. That was in Opole and in Wrocław in
           1962. Then we played it everywhere. We performed it for a
           long time, from 1962 until 1970, eight years.

Campo: *Considering the huge number of rehearsals and the kind of*
           work you were doing, which must be always precise and iden-
           tical each time, how could you still find the Life and not be
           mechanical? It is a very classical problem of the actor. How
           did you solve that problem?

Molik: It could never be the same. It depends on the day, it depends
           on the weather, it depends on your own feelings and so on. It
           was never the same, it is never the same.

Campo: *Grotowski was present at most of the performances. He said*
           that when he heard, when he felt that a performance was dead,
           he cancelled it, he stopped playing it.

Molik: I don't remember these episodes, but maybe he did cancel the
           performances and we didn't know why. If he said that, yes, it
           is possible.

Campo: *You created your own techniques, you always preserved the*
           freedom of the performers, also of your students, and you
           worked directly with the energy found in the natural environ-
           ment and your other workplaces, and you still do. What, then,
           is the role of tradition and the past? Do you feel any connec-
           tion with tradition?

Molik: For me, I may say that tradition is *res sacra*. These are my
           words, so I don't know what more I can say.

Campo: *What about the transmission of knowledge?*

Molik: Whose knowledge?

Campo: *For example, your knowledge.*

Molik: My knowledge. When I start a new work I don't use any knowledge.

Campo: *Do you think that texts can transmit some knowledge?*

Molik: No, I would say that they don't. For me a text is always just a text, you must deal with it, yes, but you can't get much from it. 'Words, words, words', as Shakespeare said, and for me the same, nothing else, nothing more. What is important is what you give and bring to that text, and you must put into it all of your life. This is important, exactly what I'm saying now: you must give and bring to the text your whole life, your whole experience, the whole tradition, all your sufferings, all your joys, everything! You must put your actual self into the text and then yes, it can be really alive. I was once at a performance of *Hamlet*, Hamlet was played by a very well known actor, *renommé*, it was in a good theatre, in an old theatre, in Cracow. I couldn't understand a single sentence he said, nothing, because it was so empty; there were 'words, words, words', exactly, and he was a so-called 'good actor', a very 'good actor', a teacher in the Theatre School. I don't know how he did it. I didn't understand a single sentence, nothing. I was deaf, it was so empty. I could hear the others, yes, but him, not. Huf! For that reason he was a genius!

Campo: *Many people who watch the films taken of the Theatre Laboratory's performances want to know the meaning of the text and they ask me: 'please explain the text'. Their attitude is that if they don't follow the text they believe they will miss the essence of the performance. I say to them what's really important is just to try to get all that we can from experiencing the images and the sound, but all they want are the words. Many people grew up watching the videos of Grotowski's performances without being able to understand a single word of the text, and even though the quality of the images were also very poor, this somehow didn't negatively affect our experience of them. On the contrary, these videos were very fascinating for us. Now we have a beautiful new edition of the film of* The Constant Prince*, digitally restored with the subtitles in many languages including Polish, because even for a Pole it isn't easy to follow the text, the actions, the emotions etc. when everything is happening so quickly. But now with this edition I must say that* *it's very interesting to be also able to understand the meaning of the words.*[2]

Molik: Of course, this is absolutely necessary to understand, to have a clear text, but without Life it always means nothing. You should see Arnold Schwarzenegger in Czech, it's so funny for us, you can't imagine how funny.

Campo: *I was also thinking of other kinds of texts, not just literary or dramatic ones that you can use directly as a performer. But instead the texts of Stanislavski about his own life, work and research, or just to remain strictly in the field of theatre, texts like* Towards a Poor Theatre,[3] *or* The Theatre and Its Double[4] *that are full of vision. Texts made by the masters, written in such a way and by someone who basically wanted to transmit his experience (which eventually can become knowledge) so that the reader could theoretically get something from the author. What do you think about these texts? These function in the same way as some of the holy scriptures, where the text itself is something which supposedly constitutes some knowledge, no matter what topic it deals with, is related to, when it was written and in what kind of society or culture.*

Molik: In that case the text is very important. Sometimes it can be that way, or the other way around. At times the text is not important, it's just relatively important and at other times the text itself is very important and the rest is not important, so it's the contrary. It depends on the context, of course. I mean, in a way the text is always important, but sometimes it isn't as important as the Life itself.

Campo: *Do you know other methods of transmitting the knowledge?*

Molik: Other than words? Of course, for example pantomime,[5] or some singing.

Campo: *How can the real experience of real life pass from one individual to another?*

Molik: There are ways, but certainly the text is not the only one. Very often it is one of the main factors, but not always.

Campo: *Although you had some good teachers, would you say you learnt everything by yourself when you started, and you were, in a way, self-taught?*

Molik: I think so.

Campo: *I'm sure you have met many good actors and perhaps some real masters, but certainly some very good performers. Did you learn anything important from your experience with these practitioners?*

Molik: Well, it certainly happened that some of them were for me a kind of inspiration, but that's all. If it happened that you saw or heard some good actors, certainly you would ask yourself: 'What good can I take from them?' Certainly there were such cases, but I don't remember them.

Campo: *What was the role of Zavatzky, the teacher who continued Stanislavski's and Vakhtangov's work, who Grotowski studied under? Was there anything that came to you indirectly from the Stanislavski tradition through Zavatzky? Or was that tradition just one of the sources that you utilised? This idea of the lineage was always present in Grotowski's mind; maybe this is one of the reasons why he went to study in Moscow.*

Molik: I think I can give you an example: just before leaving the theatre school a professor told me that it isn't important what you've learnt in the school, but it is important who you were there with. I mean, with whom you have dealt, who you had contact with, who influenced you. That's the most important thing, not how much someone has taught to you.

Campo: *Maybe those who posed questions, problems, to you were important; those who made you think.*

Molik: It was important who influenced me. For example, in the theatre school there were two people who influenced me. These were masters for me. Later in life I had only one master, and that was Grotowski, quite simply. I must say it because it was true.

Campo: *What about Artaud?*

Molik: It was already in the sixties when I found an article about Artaud somewhere in a review and I gave this to Flaszen and Grotowski, and then they started to be interested in him. They had never heard anything about him before this episode.

Campo: *Why did you decide to enter an acting school?*

Molik: I felt lost. I didn't know what to do with myself.

Campo: *You were young.*

Molik: Young, yes, but not so young, in fact it was after three attempts to study. I started twice at the Academy of Physics, and I tried law twice. I've got the academic transcripts from that time, and three before I entered the Academy of Theatre. I tried, but I couldn't complete.

Campo: *You weren't allowed to enter the school, or you just couldn't continue?*

Molik: I couldn't go on. I entered easily and I passed the exams easily, even the second time. There were some problems because I had lost a year and I tried to complete the first year again and it wasn't easy, but I managed. It wasn't because I was indolent, it was because I was seeking the whole time for something that could really involve me, something that could be really interesting for me. I didn't have the patience for law; I liked it very much but I had no patience.

Campo: *You didn't have a passion for theatre before that time?*

Molik: No, it was something concrete that happened. I met a friend of mine, a girl, at a time when I felt lost. She told me that a new department was opening, the Theatre School, in Warsaw. I finished my military service after two years and I went there for the exam, still in uniform, and I passed. I was taken on and then I started, but it was purely by accident that she told me about the school, a pure accident that I met her before I went to do my military service, because at the time I felt completely lost after three attempts to study.

Campo: *You didn't have to do military service; was it your choice?*

Molik: I didn't have to, yes it was my choice, but when I got the invitation I accepted it. I still remember Captain Leopold Kozłowsky, who needed a *conférencier*. He pulled me out of the army after three months (after which time I was absolutely obliged to stay) and brought me to his ensemble choir. Later I spent almost two years in this ensemble, the ensemble of the Polish Army. He had to tolerate me because nobody else could say his name so well.

Campo: *How old were you?*

Molik: I was twenty-one.

Campo: *And how, why did it happen? Were you already singing? Why did he choose you?*

Molik: After my decision not to refuse the call from the army I did the normal compulsory military service. The first three months I had to be a real soldier, a *Rekrut*; the first months are a very hard time. Later – instead of me serving regularly the two years of normal service – my mother went to Captain Kozłowsky and told him what a good artist there was in the Army. I was already an artist, because before going into the Army I worked for one year in an artistic agency as *récita-teur*, someone who recites poems: that's how I kept myself. I started working when I was twenty, already as a kind of actor, without any knowledge of the actor's work. That is how I started working in theatre. A colleague taught me a poem and with this poem I went to an agency that needed new people who could recite poems well. I started in the streets, outdoors, I was travelling a lot. I even went to the far eastern regions of Poland to recite some very popular poems about the hard conditions of life. People from the small villages were weeping, weeping, when I was saying these moving words. These were very simple people. My mission at that time, with a small ensemble of five people, with an accordionist, another musician and two singers, a tenor and a soprano, was to gather people from these small villages in order to build the Nowa Huta, the new big factory for steel, near Cracow. It was a big factory for steel and those kinds of things; actually it wasn't just a factory, it was also a big enterprise. They needed people, because there were not enough workers as it was very big, and in Cracow there were no people, they needed workers. So they employed this artistic agency whose name was Aktors, where I was already working sometimes, and the agency sent us there to mobilise people to go to work there in the Nowa Huta, which means the New Metallurgy. So basically, we gave performances to create publicity for people to go and work in this big factory, just next to Cracow. That's how I started my artistic career, and from being with musicians, with singers all the time, I became interested in voice and so on. So I wasn't a waiter before I was an artist, because normally in Hollywood artists start as waiters. I never was a waiter. Sometimes things work differently. Anyway, I was the assistant of a truck driver when I decided to go to the theatre school. That was my work, to help the driver of a big truck. Isn't it funny?

Campo: *When you were in the Army were you singing in the choir as well?*

Molik: Not too much, I was, rather, the *conférencier*. There's a funny story about it: one time the chief of the orchestra took me because he wanted to include me in the choir, this big choir with lots of people. I could never in my life be as big an actor as I was there. My exam was fantastic. I failed every note perfectly. I sang all of the notes perfectly falsely.

Campo: *You did it spontaneously, because you didn't have a specific preparation.*

Molik: No, I did it on purpose so as to not be included in the choir.

Campo: *Make me understand; you sang all the notes wrong because you didn't want to sing in the choir?*

Molik: Yes, instead of a clean 'ah' I did it this way: 'aha/aha/aha' with a sort of tremolo. I did a show, like never before in my life.

23

Campo: *But why didn't you want to be part of the choir?*

Molik: Because I didn't want to be busy with the rehearsals for four hours a day. During that time I could lie on my bed and play guitar and sing a little the songs I wanted, and read the paper or books.

Campo: *Funny stories. Would you like to recall something about your family and your parents? The kind of family it was, what your feelings toward your family were during your childhood and afterwards, the kind of environment you lived and grew up in.*

Molik: Of course. I remember with love my mother, my father and my sister, who is still alive. It was a normal family. I was from a simple family, with some roots, so I'll tell you a story about where the name Molik comes from. You see, my father, my grandfather and my great-grandfather were all born in a small village not far from Cracow. When Napoleon was returning from Moscow he had a violinist with him, his name was Henry Molique. This violinist broke or wounded his leg and he had to stay there, in my family village, for a certain period of time. He liked the place and when he was better he met a Polish girl and married her, and in that way my family was created. This is my story. I read a little paperback about music and it is a matter of fact that this guy existed and his name was Henry Molique and he was a violinist and he was with Napoleon in Moscow. Therefore it could have happened that he became ill and stopped in this small part of the countryside, which isn't even a village, just a small peasants' place.

Campo: *And it remained as a peasants' place.*

Molik: Yes, it still exists as a small village, very small, with less than fifteen houses.

Campo: *Were you a family of workers?*

Molik: No, peasants. My father left and came to Cracow. My mother came also to Cracow from the east side of our country and they met in Cracow, and they lived in Cracow together until the very end.

Campo: *You grew up in a town and not in the countryside.*

Molik: Yes, I was in Cracow all the time. I was born in Cracow.

Campo: *So you never had this close contact with nature, in which domain a peasants' culture could help you.*

Molik: I have had some contact because when I was a little boy I used to visit my grandparents in that little place. It's thirty kilometres from Cracow and I visited them very often when they were alive.

Campo: *In a famous picture we see you playing the violin. It was taken during the rehearsals for* Akropolis. *Did you really learn how to play the violin just for* Akropolis?

Molik: Yes. But first I played the guitar, when I was in the Army.

Campo: *So you studied music.*

Molik: No, I did it privately, for pleasure. I just tried to learn and play by myself. I studied some history of music later, in the theatre school, so I know something about music.

Campo: *And for* Akropolis *you did the same, on your own, without a teacher?*

Molik: Yes, I learnt by myself. I knew three or four melodies, and I learnt how to play them. One was 'Tango Milonga', a piece from very popular folk song.

Campo: *All Polish themes.*

Molik: No, in *Akropolis* I also played something taken from some operetta.

Campo: *That was because you liked opera and operetta.*

Molik: Yes, I liked them very much. Besides, I had a lot of contact with it, I watched them a lot because in the Army ensemble there was the opera or the operetta once a week.

Campo: *What happened after the theatre school, what was the next job?*

Molik: Afterwards it was normal, I entered the theatre. First in Łódź, where there is a famous film school, and then in Opole, the year after, where Grotowski found me because he was establishing the theatre there with Flaszen.

Campo: *Grotowski was also fresh out of school.*

Molik: Yes, almost.

Campo: *So one year after you finished school you went to Opole.*

Molik: Yes, after one year of work in the theatre in Łódź I went to Opole.

Campo: *You were working in an institutional theatre there.*

Molik: Yes. Then Grotowski found me because we knew each other from the summer camp of the theatre schools.

Campo: *How did you deal with the institutions? In a way that system gave you the chance to work.*

Molik: Yes, there was no problem. There was a lot of work after the theatre school in Warsaw, in many theatres in the province. In Warsaw or in Cracow there were problems getting accepted directly after the school, but in the other towns you could normally be accepted without problems.

Campo: *And then how did you develop your relationship with the institutions? What happened over the course of the years?*

25

Molik: Practically, once I had connected with Grotowski I stayed with him all the time until 1985. Except that I took a 'holiday' after two or three years of work with Grotowski. I was so tired that I went back to the normal theatre in Cracow. I was physically, completely exhausted. It was very hard work because I had to play the main roles all the time. Only later Cynkutis and Cieślak came and started playing the main roles. Until then I was the only one, practically the only professional one in the company. It was funny.

Campo: *They also came from acting schools or drama departments. All actors were more or less professionals, when they started working with Grotowski. They all had their own foundation for acting.*

Molik: No, not all of them, but Cynkutis and Cieślak, yes.

Campo: *I would like to know something more about the relationship with the institutions. Eugenio Barba⁶ told of an episode about some problems you had with the Communist Party: they wanted to close the theatre and so you had the idea of entering the Party so that they couldn't close the group because you belonged to the Party. Do you remember that episode?*

Molik: Yes, it did happen. I do remember.

Campo: *So you had lots of problems, especially at the end (maybe not so many when you were just a theatre company) but certainly after the paratheatrical period. In fact Grotowski decided to leave because he wasn't feeling secure or safe. There was martial law. Jairo Cuesta has told that the group of Theatre of Sources during that time had to live for months shut in the room on the ground floor of the building in Wrocław.⁷ However, overall what do you think of the old system and what do you think of the Western system, both at that time and now? Do you think that now there are more opportunities and chances than before, especially considering your kind of work?*

Molik: I think that now there are much fewer chances than before to do such a thing as Grotowski did, because now life is so much more commercialised. Everything is commercialised. At that time it wasn't easy but it was possible, but now I don't believe that it is really possible to create such a company and go on with it.

Campo: *You said Grotowski was a master for you.*

Molik: Yes. Right.

Campo: *What is the quality that allows you to say: 'This is a master'? Who is a master?*

Molik: Someone who can inspire you spiritually. But professionally Grotowski wasn't my master because I was already formed. In a human spiritual sense, yes, he was a master, a real master. I would go into the fire with him, so to say, yes.

Campo: *You really trusted each other.*

Molik: Yes, he was a real master for me. But my idol was a man called Kasimir Rudzki. He was the dean of the department in the theatre school that I was in. He was a fantastic man. He was a fantastic, witty man, full of the best kind of humour. He was a fantastic man as a teacher and as an actor, and let me say he was of a very specific kind. As a person he was great, a great man, a beautiful *conférencier* in the cabaret, for example, the best of our epoch.

Campo: *He was famous.*

Molik: Yes, very famous.

Campo: *Was he your teacher as well?*

Molik: Yes, he was also my teacher, he was the dean but also a teacher. His teaching was based on something difficult to explain. He used to come and start speaking, telling stories about what happened to him that day or the day before, speaking for one or two hours. And it was so interesting to listen to that he could keep our attention the whole time.

Campo: *About teaching, we can say that even you don't have a proper 'method'. This is very clear when we consider that your approach is similar to that of a shaman. However, I wonder if in this instance you can still give some input, as if you were working as a teacher giving some general indications to an imaginary performer. How do you think, in a general way, a young actor should approach his profession, and what kind of techniques should he confront at the beginning of his work?*

Molik: I don't think that this is possible. This teaching is so individual and personal that no, I don't know how to give it in general terms. How could I?

Campo: *Do you think that the drama schools are a good starting point? Or can they even create more problems?*

Molik: No, I think that they are a good starting point. Yes, good drama schools can help, definitely, but the point is that there are very few good schools.

Campo: *What about the university drama departments? There are so many now, many more than before, all over the world.*

Molik: Yes, but most of them are useless. I must say it, yes, but some of them can help.

27

Campo: *And what about masters? Do you think that there are masters, now, to follow?*

Molik: It's very rare to find a master.

Campo: *And what do you think of all these people, I mean thousands of people, who started doing theatre just after having read a text like* Towards a Poor Theatre *for example? Without having received any sort of training as actors?*

Molik: No, I don't believe that is possible. It isn't a manual.

Campo: *So, if in your opinion there are just a very few good drama schools, and very few drama departments, and almost no masters, and if people can't start from books, how can the art of the performer still exist?*

Molik: The tradition. Follow the tradition. That's all. And everyone brings something new to the tradition and in this way it goes on. It's very simple. There's nothing more to say.[8]

3

THIRD DAY

Paratheatre – The Organic Life and the Process – Ryszard Cieślak

Campo: *Today I would like to talk about Paratheatre:[1] your participation in this adventure, how the paratheatrical actions were created and what the goals of the work were. First I want to ask how to create a paratheatrical action.*

Molik: It creates itself. For example, there are forty or fifty people, usually that was the case, and these people come to the studio space. At first nobody knows what to do. Then there are always two leaders from the group, though sometimes later there was only one. They change around because the session lasts twelve hours or twenty-four hours. It depends on when and in what circumstances the work is done. Let me say that there are two leaders. Then we just start walking, and the people start walking as well, and from time to time one of us makes a squat, and like this the Life begins. Nobody knows what is going on, it's just walking around, not knowing what to do; but then in one moment, in a given moment, everyone starts his own Life. Meaning that one is starting to get interested in what the others are doing. So someone squats, and from the other side someone else responds with the same action. It's difficult to say because this phenomenon is simply that Life starts. From time to time we start singing, and so the people sing with us, and then everything is silent again. Someone is chasing someone else by walking and someone else is running. It's simply Life with these people, these forty people who start their Lives. Quite simply. It's difficult to describe because apparently they do nothing. However, they start to live, and that's all.

Campo: *But when you started the action did you already have in mind some simple elements, like walking, squatting or singing at least? You, the guides, knew what to do and what was going to happen?*

29

Molik: No, I swear not, really not. It was always just a big improvisation. There were no rules. Some of us used to make some special actions, but that wasn't necessary. It was very often just walking and trying to catch the Life and experimenting with the contact between one another. Quite simply it was like that. It's impossible to describe it otherwise, for me at least. I can't say what I was doing because sometimes I was doing absolutely nothing when I was a leader. Sometimes I had to wake up the energy, although I can't say by what means I did it.

Campo: *But there were some basic rules, like silence.*

Molik: Yes, it was mostly in silence, there was no talking at all. As I said, from time to time some of us initiated some singing, but that was all.

Campo: *Did you wear any special kind of clothes?*

Molik: No, we used a so-called 'casual' style, casually dressed.

Campo: *Without shoes.*

Molik: Everyone was barefoot, without shoes and without socks.

Campo: *And with a certain time fixed in advance, like two hours or more.*

Molik: We started with twenty-four hours.

Campo: *Were you in a single studio space all the time?*

Molik: Yes, in the room, the whole time in the room, but not everybody had to necessarily stay in the room. We started with twenty-four hours. Later we changed to only twelve hours. So, as we started at 6 o'clock in the evening, we finished at 6 o'clock in the morning.

Campo: *Maybe we can talk about the specific projects so you can describe them more in detail.*

Molik: I can only speak about the Tree of People because I only took part in this project. The other projects were led by someone else, for example there was a project called the Mountain, another called the Street, where they were going somewhere in the town, to the train stations for example.

Campo: *I know something about these projects from what the members of Il Gruppo Internazionale l'Avventura (the International Group the Adventure) told me.[2] You say the Street project was created here. I don't remember any documentation of it, but it was actually created here in Wrocław?*

Molik: Yes, it was created here in our big room.

Campo: *Who was the leader at that time?*

Molik: The leaders were always changing. I usually worked with Ante Jahołkowski because we always had to be in twos, making changeovers as well, so that we had time for a short rest. For this we used another room which is upstairs, on the topmost floor, the third floor, which actually is a sort of wardrobe store. There were other places in the countryside around Wrocław where we worked. The main one was in Brzezinka; others were also abroad. Then the end of the sessions was that we would always suddenly open wide the door or the gate of these big closed spaces, so that the sunshine could get in. And we could go out all together and run, and then come back to the space.

Campo: *Suddenly the sun was invading the space.*

Molik: Yes, but it also happened at night, that in a given moment, in complete darkness, we used to open the gates and go out to do the running. I don't know how I did it, how it was possible to do it. I remember that once the night was completely dark, without any moon, and I led everybody through the forest, where there is a very narrow path. Nobody could see anything; we all just went there.

Campo: *Not even the leaders knew it very well.*

Molik: No, there was nothing to see. We just followed the path instinctively, but nobody knows how it was possible. It was just such a primary instinct; I don't know how to describe it.

Campo: *It was dangerous, but nothing happened.*

Molik: Yes, obviously it was dangerous, but nothing ever happened.

Campo: *Was there in the Tree of People any idea of teaching something?*

Molik: No, nothing. It was just, how to say, getting to know someone without knowing him, being really together without being together, without touching the others, however it functioned. At first we had absolutely no knowledge of anything, but later, with the passing of time, it was natural that we gained a sort of background to the work. When we had the first experiences of this kind we knew absolutely nothing, like the other participants. We were leaders but only by name, by rule. Actually we were there with complete non-knowledge, like all the others.

Campo: *So the leaders were not specialising in something. You were all doing the same.*

Molik: All doing the same, yes, or doing nothing, as well, because this is like life.

Campo: *And that started in the studio space at the Centre in Wrocław.*

Molik: Yes, it was born there. Only later did we do the same in Brzezinka and elsewhere.

Campo: *Is the name Tree of People related to the space? Like a tree with different spaces as branches? Where did you get the name from, what does it mean?*

Molik: Tree of People? Just a trunk with many branches.

Campo: *But were these branches the rooms of the space or was it something totally different?*

Molik: No it was just that we are one tree with many branches.

Campo: *A symbol of life.*

Molik: It has nothing to do with the tree as a tree. I remember the genealogy of the concept: when it was born, at the beginning, we named it the Beehive. The space where we were working was like a beehive. So the first name for that was *Ul* (beehive). And later it was changed to the Tree of People.

Campo: *Why the Beehive?*

Molik: Because our behaviour was like that of bees in a beehive. We were seeking any possibility to be in motion, like bees who move to and fro through the beehive and to the outside and so on; they are sometimes denser, all together, and sometimes more dispersed in the space.

Campo: *Tell me something about what you were doing with the honey. I was told that on some occasions, semi-naked, you used to pass honey from someone's finger to someone's mouth and so on.*

Molik: That was something else. We used elements like honey or bread or earth, but it had nothing to do with the Tree of People or this Beehive, it was a special project connected to some ceremonies. The fire, the meal, the bread, the earth, it was something now more connected with nature.

Campo: *Were these ceremonies invented by you or were they taken from some specific cultures?*

Molik: Taken from some cultures.

Campo: *They were real ceremonies then.*

Molik: Yes, real; but this project couldn't possibly be born in that room. It was born in some other places, mainly outdoors, and it took different names and shapes, like project *Góra*, Mountain project, and others, many others.

Campo: *I would like to go back to the voice now. What is the difference for the organism between the high pitch and the low pitch, the deep voice?*

Molik: High and deep. For me a fundament for the voice is that any voice must be taken from the base of the spine. Essentially, the basic difference is that you have to take the deep voice from the base of the spine, as well as the higher voice, but later it must be generated from the low part of the trunk to give the deep voice, and from the upper part of the body for a higher voice, or – and this is a famous case – from the nape, for the very high voice.

Campo: *Always starting from the base of the spine, which is a low part of the body.*

Molik: Yes, but you can make the voice high using the different resonators, like vocalising 'Hi' from the nape or 'Ah' using the chest resonator. If you want to achieve a very light voice, for example, you must take it from the chest, and a mixture can be made using resonators from the ribs or from the shoulders.

Campo: *How do these different voices affect the organism? In terms of vibrations, is there a difference between using a high-pitched voice and a deep voice?*

Molik: They are just different. If you sing using your back, you can give the voice with different strengths and different colours than when you try to sing from your chest or using the kind of mixture that you can achieve with the ribs.

Campo: *What do you think of Grotowski's work during and after the Theatre of Sources, when he elaborated the passage from a horizontal approach to a vertical research of the performer? Especially concerning the development of the idea of the 'Higher Connection',[3] which in practice I see is not very different from your work on voice, seeking for many hours the Life of the performer. In fact Grotowski himself later elaborated, through practice with his collaborators, the concepts of 'Body-Life' and 'Body-Memory'.*

Molik: About that I can't say much because I never took part in the Theatre of Sources and later projects.[4] I have always carried on with my own projects or with the Tree of People.

Campo: *Did you maintain contact with Grotowski, or did you cease communication with him? Did you keep in touch with him?*

Molik: I was in touch with him my whole life. Even when he was in New York I went to visit him, since I was working in Canada, and from Toronto to New York is just a short jump.

Campo: *Just to be more precise, what is the difference between the Organic Life which is found through the work, and the Process, that specific experience that Grotowski used to call the Process? Are there different levels of Life in the work?*

Molik: I will give you an explanation of the differences and the steps in the work. The Organic Life appears when your Life is practically, completely open and it has reached a stage of almost not knowing what to do; when you are trusting your own organism and only finding the right impulses and the right responses to those impulses. The condition for this to happen is the presence of the other Life, which is not so much organic, is already composed. In fact this other Life is something that comes from the structure that was prepared during the training. It is composed both on the local, meaning the physical, level and on the vocal level.

Campo: *I might say then that you use this composed Life also when you are experiencing the Process.*

Molik: In the Process and in all the Life you must have this other Life, which is not so organic but must be already composed, which means that it has a precise *partitura*, a score.

Campo: *But at the same time, is the Process a step forward from the Organic Life?*

Molik: Of course, yes. For example, in *Akropolis*, we practically all used the Organic Life on stage when it was necessary, and the rest was more or less a composition. It was a construction; everything was constructed; the Life was constructed on both levels, physical and vocal. The Organic Life appeared within the construction only when it was necessary. The first traces of a direct research into the Organic Life appeared in *Faust*, when everything was, how to say, even crazier. At that time, from the beginning of the rehearsals and from the first attempts, each actor had to find his own way to open the Life without using composition. However, they had to keep this Life, which by its nature is *sauvage*, and put it into a certain discipline.

Campo: *And in this way you reached the Life and then the Process.*

Molik: Yes, this is the way to reach the Process.

Campo: *So the Process wasn't just experienced by Cieślak, but all the actors had to work with this Process.*

Molik: When it was necessary, all the actors of the company were able to do it, to act in the Process, but only when it was necessary. And it didn't happen so often. The presence of the Organic Life, this stream of Life, of course, was absolutely necessary, but the real Organic Process appeared only from time to time in this stream of Life.

Campo: *Is there a specific way of reaching it, or is it just a matter of repetition, repeating the pattern of actions?*

Molik: No, there must be a special way. With these repetitions you can only work on some of the details.

Campo: *And what is this special way?*

Molik: I'll use a metaphor: think of a canal where the water is running, it is running, running, and that is this kind of Life, because it is running and it is contained by the canal sides. Now exactly on the top level of the water, the Organic Process goes slowly, like a quiet river. You never know what happens in that given moment when the Process comes; it is like, for example, an eruption from a volcano, with this lava coming out. Now the matter is, the next step is, when this kind of Life is found, how to discipline it, how not to kill it, not to eliminate this lava, this life-fire, and how to discipline it and push it into the right stream. I'll give you another example: it's like something that's crying out inside you, in such a manner that you never shouted, that you have never experienced before in your life; this is the Process itself. Well, you must preserve this matter that you have found inside yourself, and nevertheless make it acceptable for our culture, for adult people; because when you are a child you can just cry out 'Uah-uah-uah-uah', but as an adult with this 'Uah, Uah, Uah' you can make a song, for example. You have to make a song from this, or something like it, otherwise it sounds just like a 'Uaaaah', a childish lamentation and nothing else. You must be able to make a song or even just a speech with it later, or – and sometimes it is even possible – immediately. Probably what I'm saying sounds strange, but how can I describe the Process? It's something that is pure Life. It's the Organic Life in a pure form. We can't describe what's going on in these circumstances and how it is going. It's very difficult, I don't have a descriptive talent about what I did, what I was doing, what I am still doing.

Campo: *I wonder if there were some steps led by Grotowski that brought you to this stage, or if an individual approach was required, and each of you had to find his own way.*

Molik: I think that these things go well together. Grotowski made demands and each actor executed them. With Cieślak, he executed it personally and the rest of us had to find our own responses to his demand. Yes, it seems to me that Cieślak was like a genial instrument on which Grotowski could play his own Life while we were just normal people there. He never went so far with the others. He tried with Cynkutis at first, but with Cynkutis it didn't work, quite simply. But with Cieślak, yes, it worked.

35

Campo: *And with you?*

Molik: No, he never tried with me, not this. My role in the ensemble was a little different. I was kind of homeostatic. He called me homeostatic.

Campo: *Meaning what?*

Molik: Sometimes there was turbulence in the group. From time to time it happened like a big storm, and then I was able to influence it positively, to make it calm down. Not verbally, I didn't have to say anything.

Campo: *Just with your presence.*

Molik: This is one aspect. There is another aspect, but the other aspect doesn't matter.

Campo: *Maybe they had a special consideration for you, respect, because of your longer experience.*

Molik: This is partly true; the other factor was just that my constitution was of a certain kind, and it simply came out in my behaviour.

Campo: *Do you know why Eugenio Barba left the company after his experience as Grotowski's assistant director?*

Molik: Yes, I know, it was for political reasons. Our authorities manifested some signs of interest against him. I don't know exactly what, nobody actually knows, but anyway he didn't want to stay any longer. He felt some danger in staying here.

Campo: *Finally today, I would like to discuss another couple of topics that I find interesting. What is the role of sexuality? Objectively speaking, sexuality is a huge source of energy.*

Molik: Yes, of course, it is a huge source of energy, but also of creativity. It is obvious to everybody why many famous people at an elderly age are also impotent as creators.

Campo: *But specifically, how can this huge energy be used?*

Molik: I personally very rarely try to touch someone's sexuality. However, I did do it a few times, though not much. I don't know how many times, but let me say sometimes, a few times. Anyway I did, I touched it directly. I mean not with my senses but by stimulating it, by using some images and so on. Of course it works. It works using sexuality on the level of searching for a possible way to create more than usual; how to be more creative. Yes, this is a fact. There is no doubt that sometimes you have also to go into this region of sexuality.

Campo: *I don't know, but did Grotowski also use it in some ways in the work?*

Molik: I also don't know. But what he did with Cieślak is obvious. He had to go through it, I don't know it for sure, but from what I saw, I know that he had to go into these regions of sexuality; to the sources which everyone possesses but never uses in such circumstances as on stage.

Campo: *The last topic of the day, religion. I think too many confusing things have been said about this matter in relation to your work as a company and afterwards. I remember Ferdinando Taviani[5] saying that in a way Grotowski worked on the basis of religion without its mythology: on religious principles, on what remains of religions after you cut out the role of mythology. This idea of secular ritual,[6] for instance, could be explained in such a way. In other words, it seems that it is a sort of prayer. Technically, I mean, a prayer without the objective of the prayer, at least in its iconography.*

Molik: I would say that it was rather on the religious side, as it was seeking archetypes or some ceremonies. It had nothing to do with faith in God, certainly it is not the case. Did it rather have to do with something else?

4

FOURTH DAY

Meeting with the unknown – Montage

Campo: *I wish to talk more in depth about the roots of your work,
and your relationship to some traditions or masters. I was
thinking again about Zavatzky, or Stanislavski himself, or the
old Polish company Reduta; somehow these have influenced
your work.*

Molik: This is rather the domain of Grotowski himself. I was never
deeply interested in these problems.

Campo: *But I guess that Stanislavski in its original version was the
base for the training of all actors in Poland. It's still the way
drama schools work in all Eastern European countries, at least
because it was the official model to follow under the Soviet
regime and then became an established tradition of teaching.
Maybe for Grotowski it was something that was there, to be
used sometimes in specific ways, maybe not explicitly but as
a sort of guideline, since, as he said many times, he wanted
to continue Stanislavski's work. In synthesis, that was what he
wanted to do and what he did all his life; however, ultimately
this work on a practical level had to be done by the actors.*

Molik: Stanislavski is what I might call a big shadow, but that is all.
It was there, but I can't say that anything was taken from him
explicitly. We never really explored it.

Campo: *Not even in drama school? Was it not the approach they used
to use to teach in the schools?*

Molik: In the school some basic Stanislavskian exercises were used:
like feeling the sensations you get under the shower. This is
a very well known exercise taken from the Stanislavskian
approach. But that is all, it was absolutely incidental. We
never followed any method, there were some little things, just
some details.

Campo: *And what was specifically taken from Zavatzky?*

Molik:	Zavatzky was well known from the stories Grotowski used to tell, because he considered him his master since he had studied with him at GITIS, in Moscow. He was like a father for him, in a broad sense of the term of course, but that is all. So I only know stories about Zavatzky. It was always an indirect connection.
Campo:	*And what about the Reduta?*
Molik:	It's the same, that we only knew about it from some stories. We only knew the history of the Reduta and some episodes of their work.
Campo:	*But you had meetings with some members of the Reduta.*
Molik:	Yes, there were some meetings with a man and a woman, the Galls. They were a couple, they were married. They told us some stories about Osterwa, the director of the Reduta. They had a direct connection with him, as they were with Osterwa for a long time.
Campo:	*So your meetings with the Reduta consisted of just talking about their experiences, not real work in a studio.*
Molik:	No, just talking.
Campo:	*I was thinking of Stanislavski also because it is evident that all your work is based on precision, which was a sort of obsession for Stanislavski. Apart from the interest in precision as a concept, which I may say has become fairly common now but understood quite generically, your concrete practice in the performances was based on precision. So it would be very interesting to know the steps that you used to use for building a* partitura, *a precise score. Practically, there are many ways to build a part. However, the very evident and specific characteristic of your work which makes the difference, in comparison with other kinds of performances, is that you could repeat the score exactly, a huge number of times, and still always be able to keep the same perfect precision as well as the Life. That is, without being mechanical. So I wonder how it's possible to reach that quality. What is the difference, gap or connection between freedom and form, between improvisation and precision which coexist in this Life on stage?*
Molik:	This is a good question. But I don't know the answer. I never went deeply into these other aspects, like where a specific practice came from. I never try to define the elements of my work, of my experiences as an actor and how it went; because I was always organically following my Life, my profession. I did it, quite simply. You must seek. First of all you must seek,

39

then you must find and then you must fit it in and organise it very well. First you must find the stream of the Organic Life and then bother about how to organise it and how to make it into a form, how to make it precise. It works this way, quite simply.

Campo: *So the point is: how does one keep the freedom when one is doing it precisely? It's also the main question in our ordinary life.*

Molik: Yes, that is the question. It's always the main question while you are experiencing this kind of process. You know that all structures start, that everything started with improvisation. At least that was the way it worked with us. First it was always searching, seeking, and later, when something was found, the question was how to return to it, to its Life, how to return to the first sources, to how it was born. And afterwards, to how it was created, expressed in a certain form, and then again how to return to that form, and repeat it in order to reconstruct it. First, refind, reconstruct, and then be able to repeat it, giving at all times the full new Life to this form which had already been found once.

Campo: *And did you usually start directly from the physical actions or from other elements like character, for example?*

Molik: No, now we are talking about how to find the essence of the Life. What I call the meeting with the unknown, which always happened physically during our research, during the training or part of the training or in other circumstances of the work; when you are in an empty room and don't know what to do, waiting for inspiration, for an action. Only later do you verify whether this action that you have found could make sense or not.

Campo: *So usually all the elements of the individual work on a part would come directly from the actions rather than from a thought, an image or from the emotions. Just directly from the actions.*

Molik: Of course from the action, from the spontaneous Life, just from the action. This is what I call the meeting with the unknown. Searching for the meeting with the unknown.

Campo: *And action can specifically be used to recall memory.*

Molik: Yes, the body has its memory. It's a very well known truth. So, even if this special moment of Life lasts, for example, for just fifteen minutes, it will manifest itself in an action. It happens that when something is found, something valuable, not just anything but something which is deeply inside yourself and is somewhere but almost completely forgotten, in favourable circumstances it manifests itself in action. Afterwards you must remember what one hand was doing, what the other hand was doing, what the centre of your body was doing, what your feet were doing. Yes, then you have to gather all such details together and return in depth to this stream of small actions, and then try to return to the deep source of the action and later to make it more and more full. But first you only have to recall the design of the action, you must just remember it. And later the question is how and with what that was filled up, what the original action was filled with.

Campo: *When you work on a character, how can you keep the character in your actions and still work freely with the Life?*

Molik: This kind of research can come from one side or another side and you never know whether you are working on the character, whether you are searching for the character, or whether you are searching for the Life which is forming this character. So you don't know what you are looking for; you don't know in advance what you are searching for. I never search for the character, I search for the impulses which later could create a character.

Campo: *But where does the form that you show at the end come from? Where do you find the connection between the character and your work on creation?*

Molik: From the Life itself. From the unknown. But I must say what this Life is for me. The Life is being in the room, and having contact with the walls, having contact with the seats, having contact with the floor. It's the meeting with the unknown. It's just being in the state of looking for the unknown, making the quest for the unknown and trying to be in the unknown. And this creates the form. Step by step it creates a character through the small points, the little discoveries that you get.

Campo: *All this is very clear when I think of your work on voice and body, but I was just now thinking of the work on the performances; that's why I was focusing in particular on the work on character; the character always has some established specific elements that you need to give to the spectators, that you need to communicate. So, of course, you can search for the unknown, but bringing to it some elements of the character that must be very understandable because of the spectator's need.*

41

Molik: No. In the performance everything must be already very well known. It's like jumping – when you cross a river you look for some stones, and jump from one to another. It's exactly like crossing a river and looking for the stones for your feet. So in the performance what you have to do is to just recall how everything went the first time.

Campo: *What about the montage?*

Molik: Working on the montage is like searching for the sense of what you want to present. Let me say how it is: you have some scenes, some short scenes or some events, and then you must find the way to go, the consequences of these actions, of each one of these small points. This is the montage.

Campo: *So in this moment you start thinking of the spectator.*

Molik: Of course, in this case you must now think about the spectators.

Campo: *This means, for example, that you are taking care of the position, of the distance and the spectator's view. This is the actor work of montage.*

Molik: Yes, you have to think of everything; for example, of how to return at a certain moment from one direction and then how to go in another direction, and so on. Yes, this issue of montage is another important thing, but the essence must be lived.

Campo: *About the director's montage, I would think of cinema. I remember again Nando Taviani saying that Grotowski's work, and so also your work, as a consequence, was much influenced by cinema in terms of montage, because it's very clear that there is a very strong structure in that sense. This idea doesn't have much to do with the actual practice of cinema, but has a lot to do with cinema as a concept, as a form of art based on montage. I might say that all forms of real art are based on montage, but for films this aspect is very evident and clear, and also very influential. In fact the twentieth-century Western theatres are different from the earlier theatres for many practical reasons, but also in terms of aesthetics. This appears natural when we think that most of these theatres were created when cinema was already a powerful and established form of communication. So it's not hard to believe that Grotowski's work on performances was influenced, and so in turn your work was influenced, by the cinematographic montage. We can easily say that in your work the montage is very evident. We see that you created a net of many different foregrounds and close-ups etc., organised in a complex analogical and dialectical structure.*

Molik: Yes, that's true. Montage was very important in organising our work. Especially in the final shaping, giving the final shape to the performance. Making the montage was always a big problem, because all the time we had many different small scenes. And it changed several times before the last version. Yes, it was always hard work to create the final version of our performances. It's not like taking a normal play, let me say Chekhov's *Three Sisters*, where everything comes one after the other and you must prepare every single scene and then it is done because everything was known in advance. In fact, in such cases everything is already known beforehand and you already know how to put everything together. But in our case it wasn't like this; no, there were scenes that were cut, and then something new coming in at the last moment. So it was a much more complicated, a much more complex work in comparison with normal performances.

Campo: *I can imagine how difficult it could be putting together this kind of material. Some scenes that were particularly central to the performance had to be edited together at the same moment with others that were maybe no less significant but had less evident importance, in order to create and to simultaneously deliver different emotions to the spectator.*

Molik: Yes, that was one of the main difficulties.

Campo: *I was thinking of Eisenstein, the Russian director. He was for many reasons a revolutionary film director, especially when we take into consideration his ideas on montage. He was very important also for the theatre of his time and he left considerable documentation about it, although this part of his work is not very well studied, especially in the English-language world. He moved from theatre to cinema, bringing the same principles with him. I wonder if you believe that this is still possible, moving from theatre to cinema using the same principles.*

Molik: I think that everything is possible, so that is also possible. Nevertheless, as to the issue of montage, I would say that it is easier and more natural to go from cinema to theatre than from theatre to cinema.

Campo: *I've always wondered what the best way to make a film on theatre is, on a theatre performance for example, because usually they're bad. Just a few cases are good, like* Akropolis.

Molik: You've seen *Acting Therapy*.

43

Campo: *Yes, that is interesting, but the film from* Apocalypsis cum figuris *is a disaster. How is it possible to record the theatre, what's the best way?*

Molik: I don't know, but you have some examples. You have *Akropolis*, you have *The Constant Prince*, and then you have *Apocalypsis cum figuris*, which was a disaster, as you said. Yes, it is evident that Ermanno Olmi's footage from *Apocalypsis cum figuris* was a horror. However, the film from *Akropolis* is acceptable, and also *The Constant Prince*, even if it's not so perfect.

Campo: *Yes,* The Constant Prince *film is not professional, but still very good.*

Molik: Yes. However it was made, the fact is, it still exists.

5

FIFTH DAY
The 'Body Alphabet'

Campo: *The gestus of the actor. The gesture.*

Molik: A theatre gesture is something quite natural. It's just a specific kind of expression of the body, of the feelings, of the emotions, of the thoughts and so on.

Campo: *But the gestus isn't something like everyday life gestures. It is different.*

Molik: We have gestures both in everyday life and in special artistic expressions, like Rodin's *Le penseur*, the famous sculpture. A gesture can be like this or like that.

Campo: *In the theatre, gestures can have a particularly dense meaning, like a synthesis of something.*

Molik: Of course, a gesture is a gesture. When I want to start thinking, I take a gesture like Rodin's *Le penseur*. And what does it mean? It means what it means. Of course, in theatre there can be gestures which are composed, and gestures which are organic. Quite organic, and these I call 'natural'. But some gestures can also be composed. These kinds of gestures have a different function. Do you agree?

Campo: *Yes, I do. And what about the 'real action'? Grotowski was very concerned about it. But even if expressed in slightly different words, it was Stanislavski's main concern too.*

Molik: Real action is real action. It's not a gesture. Because when I move my arm faintly, it's a gesture. But when I want to open the space, I do a precise line, with both the arms for example. This is action, and that is gesture.

Campo: *It's related to function.*

Molik: Yes, the function. The gesture is an expression of the inner life. And the action is always directed to the outside world.

Campo: *What about these two aspects of theatre, sincerity and fiction, meaning its nature of being fake? Obviously, theatre is always*

fake in itself because it's the place where you just play some-
thing. But good theatre work is sincere. How can these two
aspects coexist?

Molik: You must create fiction with real life. In theatre you create a kind of fiction. But when you create the fiction, if you want it to be good – and it must be – it has to be true, so it must at the same time be real life. Because if it's not, nobody would believe you.

Campo: *I remember something that Maja Komorowska[1] said about what Grotowski wanted, which again is the same as what Stanislavski wanted. He always used to say to the actors: 'I believe you' or 'I don't believe you', asking you to repeat the action if wasn't believable. Is it true, is this something that he always used to do?*

Molik: Yes. Always. Once Cynkutis[2] was close to killing Grotowski with a chair, after two hours in which Grotowski kept on repeating all time 'I don't believe you'. Cynkutis was supposed to express something with his shoulders, that he was crying, but only with his shoulders, and Grotowski made him carry on for such long time, repeating 'I don't believe you, I don't believe you … ' that he exploded and was very close to killing him with the chair. Only then Grotowski said: 'Yes, now I believe you', which was like saying 'Stop!' because Cynkutis was running towards him with the chair like a furious bull, so he said 'Stop! Now I believe you!' Funny story.

Campo: *Now, changing topic completely, I would like to know some-thing about the effects of the paratheatrical practices in the actual theatre. I know lots of performers who started doing theatre after they had some experiences in parateatre. Do you think that parateatre can be useful for an actor in profes-sional terms?*

Molik: Very, very useful, and it changed the value of our perform-ances. I can say that the experiences with nature and so on completely changed our playing. I say playing because, as we were saying before, in a way an actor is supposed to play. So paratheatre completely changed our approach to playing. Even without knowing it, without being aware of it, it abso-lutely changed our approach. It wasn't the same acting before the experiences with paratheatre and after. There was a big difference. The paratheatre came while we were performing *Apocalypsis cum figuris*, and it changed all the life in the performance. This close contact with nature changed our whole organism as well. Not only the lifestyle, but also the organism changed.

Campo: *So it wasn't a matter of techniques. You had a real change; that is what you experienced through paratheatre. Your own life changed; that's why when you performed, your way of acting changed, your own presence was different.*

Molik: Yes. It's like the difference between life in town, where you are limited by streets and so on, and life in a big space, in nature, in a wide open space.

Campo: *But you used to practise paratheatre indoors also, and even in the town. So it wasn't just about contact with nature.*

Molik: Well, but we brought it in, we brought nature into town, into the room.

Campo: *So the source of paratheatre is always nature.*

Molik: Yes, of course. We weren't the same after the experiences we had with nature through paratheatre.

Campo: *Do you think that Active Culture, this new approach you invented to theatre and art, where everybody is active and there are no longer passive users, was a revolution or a continuation in the path that you were following?*

Molik: It was quite simply an evolution.

Campo: *But it is clear that everything changed. Because, for example, you stopped performing at a certain moment.*

Molik: No, we didn't stop. Once or twice a week we used to come back from Brzezinka and still perform *Apocalypsis cum figuris*.

Campo: *But then, after the long period of* Apocalypsis *you stopped. Grotowski stopped, he left.*

Molik: Practically, that was the last performance, yes. Officially.

Campo: *Do you say 'officially' because in fact, unofficially, you were doing something that wasn't shown?*

Molik: There were some attempts with Cieślak. When Grotowski left us they did this *Thanatos Polski*. Maybe also Flaszen was a little bit connected with it.

Campo: *But anyway apart from some episodes, basically all of you stopped performing shows. There was a clear cut there.*

Molik: Well it was. However there was this attempt to continue with *Thanatos Polski*. But without me. I didn't agree to take part in that project. Because I said that without Grotowski I wasn't interested in continuing with the group. It was a small scandal because I refused the role against the rules.

Campo: *Because they were all involved in that project.*

47

Molik: Yes. But I refused. At that time I led my own project with voice.

Campo: *Was Rena Mirecka also involved in that project?*

Molik: No, she couldn't be in that project. For other, different reasons.

Campo: *Now I have to ask you something very important. What I would like to know is, if after all your experiences with voice, you could individuate a precise map of points of energy in the body which is universal, identical in anybody. I understand that on the one hand it's obvious that the body structure changes for each person, but on the other hand there are lots of traditions saying that there are some fixed points in the body where these kinds of energies can be concentrated. So I wonder if you work on them and if you have ever built your own map of centres of energies in the human body. I wonder if in your work through the voice you follow this sort of map, universal for anyone.*

Molik: Yes, I think I do.

Campo: *Can you explain how it is?*

Molik: Not really. It's too complex, too complicated to explain.

Campo: *Can you try?*

Molik: No, I don't want to.

Campo: *Is this a development of the work on resonators or is it something totally different?*

Molik: No, this matter of the resonators is secondary. This is just a secondary thing, it's more outside, external, it's not the point, it's too obvious. Resonators are obvious things.

Campo: *This is the section 'Resonators' from the chapter 'Technique of the Voice' in* Towards a Poor Theatre*:*

The task of the physiological resonators is to amplify the carrying power of the sound emitted. Their function is to compress the column of air into the particular part of the body selected as an amplifier for the voice. Subjectively one has the impression that one is speaking with the part of the body in question – the head, for example, if using the upper resonator.

[The term 'resonator' is purely conventional. From a scientific point of view it has not been proved that the subjective pressure of the indrawn air into a determined part of the body (thus creating an external vibration of the spot) causes this area to function objectively as a resonator. Nevertheless, it is a fact that this subjective pressure, together with its obvious symptom (vibration), modifies the voice and its carrying power.]

In reality, there is an almost infinite number of resonators, depending on the control the actor has over his own physical instrument. We shall limit ourselves here to mentioning just a few.

a The upper or head resonator which is the one most employed in European theatre. Technically, it functions through the pressure of the flow of air into the front part of the head. One can easily become aware of this resonator by placing the hand on the upper part of the forehead and enunciating the consonant 'm', when one should be able to feel a definite vibration. Generally speaking, the upper resonator comes into use when speaking in a high register. Subjectively one can feel the air column passing through, being compressed and finally hitting the upper part of the head. When using this resonator one must have the sensation that the mouth is situated at the top of the head.

b The chest resonator, known in Europe although rarely used consciously. It functions when one speaks in a low register. To check whether it is in action, place a hand on the chest which should vibrate. To use it, speak as though the mouth were situated in the chest.

c The nasal resonator which is also known in Europe. This functions automatically when the consonant 'n' is pronounced. It has been unjustly abolished by most theatre schools. It can be exploited to characterize certain parts or even a whole role.

d The laryngeal resonator, used in oriental and African theatre. The sound produced recalls the roaring of wild animals. It is also characteristic of some negro singers of jazz (e.g. Armstrong).

e The occipital resonator. This can be attained by speaking in a very high register. One projects the flow of air towards the upper resonator and, while speaking in a continually mounting register, the flow of air is then directed towards the occiput. During training, one can reach this resonator by producing a high pitched mewing sound. This resonator is commonly used in classical Chinese theatre.

f In addition, there exists a series of resonators which actors often use unconsciously. For example, in so-called 'intimate' acting, the maxillary resonator (in the back of the jaws) comes into use. Other resonators are to be found in the abdomen, and in the central and lower parts of the spine.

g The most fruitful possibility lies in the use of the entire body as a resonator. This is obtained by using simultaneously the head and chest resonators. Technically, one must concentrate one's attention on the resonator which is not automatically in use at the moment in which one speaks. For example, when speaking in a high register, one normally uses the head resonator. One must therefore concentrate on exploiting simultaneously the chest resonator. In this case 'concentrate' means to compress the air column into the inactive resonator. The opposite is necessary when speaking in a low register. Normally the chest resonator is in use, so one must concentrate on the head resonator. This resonator which engages the whole body can be defined as a total resonator.

Interesting effects can be obtained by simultaneously combining two resonators. The simultaneous use of the occipital and laryngeal resonators, for example, produces the vocal effects achieved by Yma Sumac in her renowned Peruvian songs. In some cases one can combine two resonators, making one of them function as a 'solo' and the other as the 'accompaniment'. For instance, the maxillary resonator may give the 'solo' while a uniform 'accompaniment' is provided by the chest resonator.

Who wrote this chapter of the book?

Molik: Grotowski wrote that chapter.

Campo: *Did you have any part in realising that chapter, or was it something that Grotowski did completely on his own?*

Molik: I think that he did it on his own. Why not?

Campo: *It seems strange, because you did the work, you made the exploration of the resonators, but then the description wasn't done by you. In fact, in that chapter there are some parts on which you certainly would not agree. For example, you said that you never used the highest point, the occipital resonator, at least not in the way Grotowski used to. In fact it came from the Chinese tradition, which always fascinated Grotowski. As hinted at in the text, these kinds of exercises come from the actor training of some forms of classic Chinese opera.*

Molik: Yes, he used to play with this 'Oh-oh', with this point on the top of the head, and I was never interested in it. I already mentioned somewhere here that for me the highest place for the voice in the body is *la nuque*, the nape. Up on the back of the neck, that you can vocalise with 'Eh!' That is all. Apart from that, you can use anything. I try to use the chest, the ribs, the shoulders, and of course the lower and the middle part of the body.

Campo: *Do you think that respiration can involve all the body, from the feet to the head?*

Molik: Yes of course. The whole body must be involved. If you are in a real process the whole body must inspire, must breathe. All, from the feet, the whole body. It's difficult to explain, because we know that for respiration we are organically limited to only that part, that middle part of the body. But practically, the whole body must take part in the process of breathing. And it's right what you were saying, that it must come from the feet. From the earth. The energy must be taken very often from the earth.

Campo: *This is one of the reasons why you usually work with bare feet.*

Molik: Well, also, yes.

Campo: *The Chinese Taoists say that we can breathe from the centre of the palms. Actually I do it often, because it works. So I know that there are some specific centres in the body from where you can breathe the energy.*

Molik: I never tried with the palms. But I believe them. Because the Chinese are very specific people and certainly they can do it with the palms. I never tried, but maybe that's also a good way to do it.

Campo: *They also do it from the feet, and taking the energy from the feet is something that you also use.*

Molik: Yes. I have used this since the very beginning.

Campo: *Which is what specifically? The centre of the feet or the feet as concept?*

Molik: We can say I rather use it as a concept. Because we don't know exactly where the energy comes from, whether from one part or another of the feet. Sometimes it comes from the heels, other times from the front part of the feet. It depends. But anyway, there is a connection with the earth. So, they must be alive and they must be like conductors. Conductors of the energy of the earth.

Campo: *What about the head? Traditionally it is connected with the air.*

Molik: The head, in my opinion, as far as I am concerned, should be eliminated. It's never possible to eliminate the head completely, but I always try to eliminate the head.

Campo: *I mean the head not as intelligence, I mean physically.*

Molik: Yes, physically. The intelligence can stay there, but only as spirit. Intelligence is part of the spirit. And all that's physical in the head should be eliminated, for me.

Campo: *It's time to speak about voice in relation to actions and movements. We've talked already about the origin of the voice and the way the voice can work in itself; now I wonder about the relation between voice and actions and movements.*

Molik: I can only say that too much action is not good for the voice. But some actions are necessary.

Campo: *Are you thinking of anything specific?*

Molik: Yes, in a given moment you must be able to do the action, the right action of the body in order to get the right sound. But if you do too much, the energy is dispersed. And then the voice is empty, it gets empty. So you must be very careful about it. You must be very prudent if you need a great amount of actions. If there are many actions you need to be very watchful not to disperse the energy and to keep it in one single source. Be conscious of the risk of losing energy while you are performing many actions.

Campo: *So in order to keep the energy it is possible to concentrate all the energy in one point and use it as a reservoir.*

Molik: For the sound. And make only the minimum use of the energy for some necessary gestures. If, for example, there are not actions but gestures to be performed. Don't disperse the energy for useless actions, for useless gestures.

Campo: *Is there a way to recharge the body of energy and to keep the energy in the body in certain moments of need of the voice?*

Molik: For the sound, yes, but sometimes this is connected with a concrete action, a concrete body action. How is it possible to charge the voice? When you need to lift up a heavy thing, you must charge your body in order to do it. So the same is with the voice. You must focus, concentrate the energy in this part in which you need to create a specific sound.

Campo: *So the way of charging depends on the specific use of the voice that is required by the situation. So there is not just one way of charging.*

Molik: There are millions of ways. For each moment there is a different way of charging.

Campo: *When we say 'theatre of research', which is an ugly term, but quite common, what do we mean, what do we research and why?*

Molik: It depends on what we want and why we want it. Very often we don't know why, but we need to research. And we don't know what we are concretely searching for. It can also happen this way. But sometimes we know very well what we want to find, and so why we are searching, but we don't know how to do it.

Campo: *What is the value of the group in a research? What is the value in itself of some people working together? If there is one.*

Molik: There is one. You mean in comparison to when you are seeking alone, searching alone.

Campo: *About the laboratory theatre, Grotowski used to say that it's a place where we can get rid of the weapons, as opposed to everyday life, which is a hard life, always wearing weapons and masks out of necessity. I think the laboratory theatre can be a sort of creation of a new world. More precisely, it's the possible condition for experiencing a different level of life.*

Molik: Maybe he meant that in such place we're obliged to research but we are not obliged to find. While in our ordinary life we are obliged to find something. In the form of a *laboratorium*, we are free.

Campo: *Grotowski used to criticise the capitalist system, the mercantile system and the United States in particular. In fact he ran away from the USA and went to a sort of poor place in Italy, and this is very well known. I know you have a similar approach, so I wonder if this directly influences your work. For example, I have read a radical criticism you made of some English people you had to teach. It was in 1981. You said something quite harsh to Jennifer Kumiega, in an unpublished interview, about these English pupils you had. You said you couldn't work well with them, that they were worse than some Australian or even North American participants. I wonder if you have changed your opinion about it. It's very interesting because your influence on British theatre is quite strong. Apart from some evident misunderstandings, and although you have been in Britain just a few times, your influence on this culture is strong. Nevertheless, in this interview you say very clearly that the worst pupils you have ever had were English or British. Mainly English.*

Molik: I can't remember now. Maybe it was just provoked by the situation, or just by an incident, one of the two. Maybe it was something else, but it probably happened that first we worked with some French people, who are more open and free. And the English could be stiffer. I don't know exactly how to say it, not so open, not so soft. So the word is 'stiff', I believe.

Campo: *Do you think art is subjective or objective?*

Molik: I think it is both. It is objective and subjective. How could it be otherwise? No, it could not be otherwise; it is at the same time subjective and objective. Certainly art, pure art, is more subjective than objective, as far as I see it.

Campo: *You work with many subjects; they appear all the time, and they are very different. Nevertheless you always push all of them towards a specific direction that is the search of pure Life, the real Life. Which is something objective, in the end. So it looks like a linear process, from the subjective to the objective.*

Molik: Sure, it is.

53

Campo: *How to feel the objectivity at the end of the process, when the work is concluded and shown? Is it something that anybody can see, or just those who have a specific long experience?*

Molik: I don't see any reason to bother about it. Is it important for us if it's objective or subjective? For me it's never important. When I do something subjectively it must be objective. In the end. So why worry and bother about whether what I do is objective or subjective?

Campo: *Do you think that the Process, I mean that specific performer's experience that is called 'the Process', or the work in the domain of Art as Vehicle, which is its natural development, does transform the human? Does it modify once and for all the inner self of the person who experiences that, or is it just something temporary? Is it just a strong experience of one moment of your life or is it something that changes your life?*

Molik: It depends. Because it's both like this and like that. If it's experienced in a way that the same process is repeated many times, then it objectively can change the person. But if it is not, if it's done in order to have one or two experiences, it changes the self only temporarily. It works in this way.

Campo: *There is a moment before starting a performance when there is a change inside yourself, like a 'click'. Because before you are in everyday life, and then you are on another level. Stanislavski worked a lot on it, with this idea of 'spiritual toilette'. So what does happen there, and what to do?*

Molik: It's the time when you leave behind all that happened during the day and you start opening an empty space in your head so as to be ready for a new life. It's like saying 'goodbye' to the old life waiting for the new life, which is to come. I see it this way, it's quite simple.

Campo: *And what to do in order to empty yourself?*

Molik: Nothing. Just calm down and relax well and seek some serenity. Pictures, nothing heavy, just seek heaven.

Campo: *So it's not necessary to do some training and a warm-up.*

Molik: This is another thing. If you need it, you can do some warm-up. But not a heavy one, just some stretching. You can eventually lie down in some positions. It depends on how you were feeling before. If you feel tired you can do just some relaxation exercises. If you feel heavy, you do something to wake up the body. It depends.

Campo: *And for the voice?*

Molik: For the voice it's better not. Not to touch. For the voice, if someone feels it is good, they can do some warm-up, but a few hours before, at midday or in the early afternoon. Just before the performance isn't good.

Campo: *You told me that you with all the company used to stay just in silence together for twenty or thirty minutes before every perform-ance. And that was all. You never did any sort of theatrical ritual as is used in the normal institutional theatres, like some typical gestures, some words. In fact theatre people in every country have their own typical sentences and gestures. But for you there was just silence until the beginning of the performance.*

Molik: Yes, silence. This was the best for us; we did it all the time. At first it was obligatory. And later it became usual. We got so used to it that we felt we should be silent. But it was no longer obligatory.

Campo: *I wonder if you can describe some specific exercises for the voice.*

Molik: They always change depending on when and on what occa-sion, in what circumstances they are done. Whether you have an empty room, when you can receive just an echo, whether you are in a small room where you are allowed to do such things like exercising with singing in a low volume, keeping the mouth closed, singing with a low voice, etc.

Campo: *With which part of the body?*

Molik: The whole body. From the base of the spine, moving slowly and circularly the low part of the body, singing whatever and moving the trunk, the spine, the shoulders, the ribs. Just that.

Campo: *And feeling the vibrations moving up and down, this is the idea.*

Molik: Yes. And also from the feet sometimes. And also waking up the legs and the pelvis.

Campo: *This is in a small space. And what about when you are in a big space, as you were saying before, in an empty room with an echo?*

Molik: If you are interested in it, you can still use the same elements in the whole space as well, just for seeking the vibrations, the resonances.

Campo: *With a higher tone, a higher volume?*

Molik: No. Never with a high volume. You should work with the medium level.

Campo: *What about exercises in pairs, with a partner or in a group? There are some interesting exercises that can be done working with groups.*

Molik: Yes, I could tell you many stories. But you know well that I have the 'Body Alphabet'. It means that there are around thirty actions from which I construct a kind of body language. You must learn these actions by heart and then improvise the Life with these. For half an hour during the warm-up you create the Life with these actions, together with the others. The people who work with me learn them off by heart in two days. They must learn by heart these actions with which they later construct whole sentences and the whole speech of the body. They live like that, they move using these actions. How could it be otherwise? Just jumping around and what? They use the actions.

Campo: *In my film on the 'Body Alphabet' the actions are very well executed and analysed, but it is still individual work. From the other videos shot with groups,* Acting Therapy *and* Dyrygent *('The Conductor'), there is no way to get the actions; the concept is clear but the actions are not.*

Molik: Yes, it is difficult, because from these actions later on they construct the Life. There you only see moving silhouettes, and they seem not to change much, but if you look closer you would see that they do the actions all the time, with the arms, with the hands, with the pelvis, with the legs, with everything. There is the full 'Body Alphabet' even in these unclear films. Every action has a precise design. I'll give you a description of some sequences, for example, pulling. First I pull back the body of the partner using both the arms, then I do it with some steps, and then I change partners and the way of pulling, doing it laterally, from one to another, and then forward. Then I change exercise, using the arms rhythmically and raising them like wings, as if I was flying. And then I do the same with some steps, changing the partner, changing direction. Then I move the arms rotating the shoulders. And so on and so on, and then the head, I do some rotations of the head and work with the head, rhythmically coordinating these movements with the impulses that push forward the chest. There are around thirty-five actions, considering also some intermediate actions necessary to pass from one to another. Some are more complicated, like pulling the bell. Some people made a list of the exercises with some comments, but with many errors, many faults. For example, instead of indicating to go up they noted that you must go down. The opposite. I remember that a girl did it once, around five years ago, and it was terrible.

Everything was the contrary, instead of 'up' she noted 'down', and so on and so on. For example, the way of breathing. Because it isn't just the arms, the feet or the hands, but it is complex. It's difficult to show, to draw, and to write about it, I'm afraid, and the results are always cheap. These are very simple exercises. Simple to do, to feel, but not to speak about. The problem with my workshops is that there is no one to continue the work, apart from one man, Jorge Parente, from Portugal, who lives in Paris. He will be my successor. He's now mastered everything and he knows everything precisely and he can do it now. And he did it, he tried alone and he's OK, yes. So *nomo nis moriar.* I will not die totally. I will leave a successor. It isn't just about the Alphabet, but also because of some work he's doing with the voice with some Georgian chorus and the fact that he works individually with each person. So he follows my way of teaching well. This is the basic structure of the Voice and Body workshop: everybody has one song and one text. And they find the Life after experiencing the 'Body Alphabet'. And they wait for a special moment and they try to do something. But I only know what to say to help the participants. Because it is complex: Alphabet, voice, songs, etc. And then they do it, first individually and then all together, with the full Life, voice and body.

Campo: *Do you have any further comments to do with watching Jorge Parente in the film I shot in Paris?*

Molik: In the beginning he should be more fluent, without stops.

Campo: *A normal sequence can start from Pulling and then Pushing, as he did.*

Molik: Yes. Then, Lifting up. Then that movement of the head, that exercise with the chest and the neck, is important for opening the larynx.

Campo: *And the neck works independently from the body.*

Molik: Yes. You must work only on that point of the neck, just to open it, to lower the larynx and open it. In the other movement, Touching the sky, we have to concentrate the attention on the elbows, which should go straight, taking care not to bend them.

Campo: *To make them curves, so that the spine can be fully and correctly stretched.*

Molik: Yes. Taking the energy from the feet and then, paf! Straight up. Then, in the other exercise, going down and up, the upper part of the body, the chest, the trunk, should not be too high, but at 45 degrees. Then, Pulling the bell must be done two or three times, on the floor, like a boat. Each time must be precise: paf, paf, paf.

Campo: *That's mainly done for the back.*

Molik: Yes. Then the Butterflies, that are seeking the right flower to sit on, and looking around at what's going on.

Campo: *So the images have a very strong function, a huge part in this work.*

Molik: Yes, of course. Nothing is mechanical. Everything must be connected with the real Life. Like the next, Flying.

Campo: *To do it well is the result of hours of work.*

Molik: Well, yes. Like Jorge Parente, who's done lots of sessions with me, maybe ten. Full workshops. I nominated him my official assistant. I gave him an official diploma, to say he is a Master already. Because he actually is. Then there's the Cobra, looking around above the grass what to eat, something fine to eat. The hips are connected to the ground and the chest goes up and rotates.

Campo: *The body gets ready to do something. From the bottom of the spine to the upper part.*

Molik: Yes, it goes up. Then Shooting into the sky with the arms. Here the energy comes from the back of the hips. But at the same time you stretch the arm, touching the sky with the hand. Then, the Game with the feet.

Campo: *This is a very good exercise, because it helps the memory as well.*

Molik: It works on the muscles of the belly first.

Campo: *But also on the memory, because in a way it puts you in a very specific creative condition.*

Molik: Yes, it puts the action into real Life. When you work in the space, and change one foot after the other, one after the other and so on, it just goes organically. You don't anticipate what will be next.

Campo: *You're just present in the moment. It induces awareness.*

Molik: Yes indeed. Then with Walking to see behind you, you stretch the muscles of the groin.

Campo: *Here also the torsion of the trunk helps to open the voice.*

Molik: Yes, everything is conceived on the basis of serving the voice. All these exercises are done to serve the voice. I just conceived them in that way, the whole 'Body Alphabet'.

Campo: *This is the result of many years of research, for you. I guess it happened that way: sometimes during your work, in different stages of it, you've found something particularly effective for the voice, you've experimented with something exceptionally useful and then you've put it in the Alphabet.*

Molik: Yes, exactly, because it has nothing to do with gymnastics, or even with pantomime. Although some elements could have come from pantomime. For example, a Walk by the water is taken rather from pantomime. But it's done in such a way that it is essentially work on the hips, because the sound must be taken from the base of the vertebral column, of the spine. The arms should not be too high, but on a level with the hips. So everything must be constantly ready for its aim. Others, like Running on the spot, are conceived just to move the body, to relax all muscles, so that nothing is done by force, but just organically, like puf, puf, puf. Then Trying to touch the wall with the pelvis. Just trying, because it's impossible to touch the wall with the pelvis and the hips if the position is taken correctly. The elbows shouldn't be too bent, but rather extended as far as you can keep the right distance with the arms, which is not to be too close to the wall, so that you can move and rotate the body. Then, Jumping in the whole space, not around but traversing the space. Then, Playing with the kite.

Campo: *What is this exercise exactly?*

Molik: The kite. The kite is in the sky and is playing with the wind. And you play with the kite. It's a gentle action, not a strong, full action, but is just to give in, all of yourself, to the wind.

Campo: *I know it's very important, I worked intensively on it also with Rena Mirecka. She always makes you connect the mind and the body, the emotions and something else. Working with her is an amazing experience, involving all aspects of your being. So, after having performed the whole Alphabet, you can make a personal physical montage of the movements.*

Molik: Yes. First you must start slowly, and then go faster. And you go either in the water, for example, or on unknown terrain where one is seeking his way, where he can go, since he doesn't know where to go. So you look where you can advance, move forward, put in effort or rather be in the water, above the hips. Feeling the pressure of the water. You have your own images, for example pulling can be fighting with a horse, maybe, who knows, or maybe with the lianas, the water plants, by the water. And then try to fly. This is normally done in the whole space with all the people, under the ceiling. I often say: 'be high under the ceiling'.

Campo: *The presence of the other participants of course influences your movements.*

Molik: Of course. But anyway, in the video that you directed we see Jorge Parente doing the precise movements, even alone. He could move in a confused way and do nothing, but no, instead he takes energy from the feet and the whole body and everything is organic.

Campo: *Sometimes I see particular expressions on his faces. Are they part of the movements?*

Molik: In a way yes, because he is somewhere, in another world. There's another world for him now, something is coming to him and he's trying to find the right reaction for the new situation.

Campo: *In his improvisation he made an interesting montage, because every time he enters the following positions, in a very smooth way he's still ending the preceding ones.*

Molik: Yes, sometimes you see in his eyes that he is thinking of what must be next now, but he never stops. He's just thinking of what can be now and then he finds it. The energy goes on. Yes, he didn't get the diploma for nothing. He can really do it. I watch the video with great pleasure. And in the part with the vocal improvisation it's visible how he takes the sound from the base of the spine, the lowest part of the spine.

Campo: *Yes, and also how the voice changes with the different movements and how they influence the sound. Something interesting happened while Heather, the film technician, and I were recording it. Initially we took a sound check, at the very beginning, and she had the headphones on and we were listening to him. And as he began to move, and he came off the floor, and he started to move and stretch, the quality of the sound started to change. It distinctly started to change, and by three-quarters of the way through the whole movements, several movements, you could hear distinct resonances in the voice. That was not present at the very beginning, and because we weren't aware that this was what was going to happen, we had to actually record the piece a second time, because it started to distort the volume. He wasn't shouting or throwing his voice, but he just generated so much energy and the resonances of his voice were so powerful that the levels that we had originally taken were just distorting. We had to actually rerecord the whole movement, because it was so powerful. And we had to pull all the levels down, and record the piece again. It was very inter-*

esting, because we didn't know that this was going to happen, and all that was taken was vibrating, absolutely vibrating. It was incredible. And it isn't a matter of volume, but of intensity. It wasn't a matter of volume at all. You could hear that it wasn't coming from his vocal organs, but coming from the feet. It was coming up and out of him, like he wasn't before, and you know, first of all it was coming from his head, which is different, but by the end it was coming through his whole body. And everything is related to the movements, comes from the movements, you could hear it changing and changing and changing. It was quite exceptional.

Molik: Because he is on his trip. He's not just singing unimportant words, but in that moment his own Life is awake. He expresses his Life, not just the melody, which is not something significant. It's impersonal instead. Anyway, independent from what he is doing, and at the same time close to it. It is interesting because he started singing just a few years ago. Before he couldn't sing. He had problems with singing for many years. He didn't have problems with the voice but with singing. He couldn't find something to sing with the Life. With the voice he had no problems. He had problems with finding the music to sing with.

Campo: *So he developed his skills on the movements and this ability together.*

Molik: Yes.

Campo: *What is particularly interesting is the transmission of the experience, which in a wider sense involves a personal work on the own 'mind', which could even eventually become a sort of transmission of knowledge.*

Molik: Yes. And in the case of Jorge Parente it is well done, I must say. And anyway this kind of work is far away from what Cieślak used to do with his exercises. Because in those, everything was very forced, if you remember well, as you can still see in that famous film on his training produced by the Odin Teatret.[3] And in this, your film with Jorge, nothing is forced, everything goes just fluently, it's fluent. All those with Cieślak were very gymnastic based, some very difficult and not for normal people. And here, in the 'Body Alphabet', everything is for normal people.

Campo: *Yes, for everybody. Well, it looks like everybody can do it, although of course the quality changes.*

Molik: Yes, but it's not that it just looks like it, it is real, because after

61

three days everyone actually does such things. Maybe not so well, because Jorge is already professional, but however they do it, everybody tries to do the same. It doesn't demand any force, any gymnastics, nothing. You are a human being and that is all, all that's required is a normal organism. Everybody can do even those few exercises that here in the film seem to be difficult. Maybe not so well, but anyway, they can.

Campo: *Something comes again to my mind about imitation and invention, in particular about how to follow a master. This is probably the only way to learn practically the art of the actor, especially in our times, since the places of training are infested by these post-modern approaches, like these 'performance studies', 'post-dramatic theories' and other academic fashions, which have as a consequence the gradual disappearance of the specific research on our art, both in theory and in practice. Now any sort of so-called 'performance' is easily accepted and is replacing the theatre almost everywhere. Grotowskian experiences such as Paratheatre, the Theatre of Sources and so on, even if distant from the theatre and the art of the actor or performer, were always in a way connected to it, and anyway never opposed but instead accompanied his interests in the art of theatre. He just went beyond and beside it, integrating through a total exploration of the human adventure, studying the 'original techniques', those needs that theatre constitutes; that is what he did with different collaborators and in different projects. Grotowskian conceptions such as the 'principle of synchronicity', as opposed to the cause and effect structure in making an action, or the 'transparent consciousness', which includes the body and the movement, with a 'loss of the ego' for a sort of rebirth to a new life, can also be experienced by a performer in certain special circumstances. So the matter is still the tradition, which in fact literally means transmission. Of course Grotowski was never orthodox in that concern and he often said he preferred the 'outsiders', the rebels who must conquer the knowledge when they feel different, even if not cursed by the others. So this research has always a direct, personal and practical relationship with the unknown, and the chosen traditions have always an element of opposition and regenerative tension within the context of the official culture. Here we are in the region of unorthodox cultures or hidden traditions, to which the art of the performer, which Grotowski himself recovered*

*after all these explorations, belongs. The matter is the differ-
ence between the horizontal transmission of culture, which is
the institutional one, giving a reproducible homogeneous and
controlled corpus of notions, and the vertical culture, which
involves an organic relationship between the master and the
pupil. The problem is how to keep this tradition alive, how it is
possible not to imitate but still to be creative, being present in
the work, not just as a copy, a reproduction of something and
someone else.*

Molik: Yes, we can consider such a question in these terms, it is very
clever. I think the answer is all in Grotowski's consideration
about Eugenio Barba, that he betrayed him but he betrayed
him well. That's all.

Campo: *I reckon that this direct transmission of the experience can
eventually become knowledge, and, especially in the theatre,
only exists as a connection between theory and practice, in a
dialectical relationship between forms and principles. How
does it function for you?*

Molik: I think that it must happen in a natural manner. If we are
together for one, for two, for three or for five days, the transmission must happen in a very natural way. Because how
would you imagine otherwise? How could it be otherwise?
That what, that I would do it consciously? I cannot do it
consciously. I do it by being together with the pupil. Together,
meaning that we are exchanging something with each other.
It is what we are doing now, I am giving something and you
are giving something back to me. And such is the process, it is
a mutual process and it goes like this. Because I do not try to
teach, I am not a teacher, I am like a guide, and I try to guide
someone, to show him a road, a path. And that is all, and he
tries to follow me, to respond to me, and transmission goes
this way. It's not like I explain a lot and the pupil gets more
and more clever, because this is not the point in our relationship.

Campo: *For Grotowski this problem of transmission was always
central as he sought the connection with Stanislavski through
his pupil. Yet according to Stanislavski it isn't possible to
teach, it's only possible to learn, if you are a good thief. Technically speaking you cannot really transmit a thing. It's a
personal challenge, in the end.*

Molik: But anyway, it can be done, as is evident on the performance
level here in the video that you have made. Everything is OK.

For me, it's like this. I can say it because I made a couple of films and nothing is so clear, nothing. As you said, one is *Acting Therapy*, and the other, the last one is *Dyrygent*, 'The Conductor'. I have done them with whole groups and the result is confusing. In these two films that I have made previously only some parts are interesting, a very few moments.

Campo: *What is valuable in these films is that there you see the group working all together, and you usually work with a group.*

Molik: Yes.

Campo: *They can help us to understand the progression of the work, let's say the structure of the workshop. Because if we watch my video, and then the films with the groups, we can get an idea of the actual sequence of the work.*

Molik: Yes, and this video you have made is scientific material, and however, everything is very organic there. I mean the model is very organic.

Campo: *It's interesting what Jorge said to me while we were recording the 'Body Alphabet'. He asked me: 'Do I have to act like Molik, giving the instructions, or like a participant, having to follow the instructions?' So I gave him more precise indications and then he did both. In fact in the first part he acts like you, showing the movements that must be followed by imaginary participants, and in the second part he acts like a participant working with them. But of course there are other steps in the work with the participants. This is just a short synthesis of the work.*

Molik: Yes, because then you have to find your personal Life, and then you must put it together with the text, and this, I might say, is another thing. For example, this Life that Jorge was singing out, in certain circumstances can be given with a text, instead of just with the open sound as he did for the film. It requires only a few adaptations, but the general design can be the same. It can be expressed with both the energy, with all the resonances, and the melody and the music. When I say with the music I mean the music of this Life, the personal creation, the music with the text, not just the melody. It should be like a song, just like what he was singing in the film. What Jorge has shown was just like a song, but then the speaking must be the same, like a song. In fact the next step is to adapt a great monologue over this music. However, the expression of this is quite different. This can't be too mild, it rather must be based on personal emotions. Afterwards you have different stages of this trip to go through. It can't be all the time the same, the same, the same as Jorge was singing. That was more or less all the same, it was just trying and improvising a certain song, toward the nature or for the nature or of the nature or something like this. But when the Life is found, when it's more personal, then that is all, it's everything. You never know how much you have to give. You must find the point where you are touching the impossible, and then give everything. I mean not by forcing the voice but by giving all yourself. You have to be like this. All your heart must be in this.

Campo: *Completely immersed in what you are doing. Totally inside it.*

Molik: Yes. You must be totally with it, with that Life. And on this Life you just live the text, instead of saying something.

Campo: *How is the memory involved in this process? I mean both the personal memory and other kinds of memories.*

Molik: Partly by the brain, partly by the body.

Campo: *Just naturally then. It just arrives. At a certain moment the memory arrives.*

Molik: Yes, when the Life is found during the improvisations, later on the body brings memories to your brain. This, that you see performed by Jorge, was a very simple Life, it was like the simple life of a plant. It was rather like a big tree. There were very slow movements of the branches, and that was all. But there was no storm there, nor rain, it was just like being on a hill during a nice afternoon and singing to the space all around. But nothing happened in this Life. But when a big storm or something like that comes, something strong that you can't take any more, like the strongest hit of the sun, when we are almost burning, then yes, it is a quite different Life.

6

IMAGES OF THE 'BODY ALPHABET'

6.1 Images of Jorge Parente performing the Body Alphabet. From the film *Zygmunt Molik's Body Alphabet*. Pulling the body.

6.2   Lifting up

6.3 Pushing forward and aside

6.4 Rotation of the shoulders

6.5 From the nape backward, the chin straight and backward, and then relax

6.6   Head play

6.7   Rotation of the head

6.8 Open the arms to the sky, everything is open, go down with the hands and
touch the ground and sharp reaction (recognising something in the ground
– a partner – which can be anything)

6.9   Touching the sky

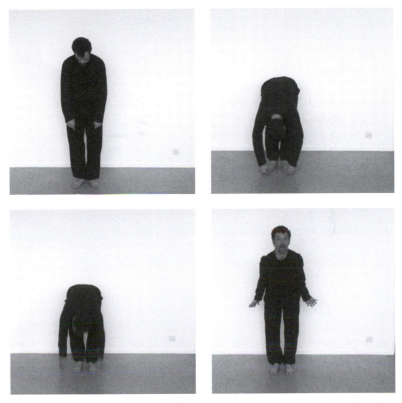

6.10 The arms are heavy and pulling down and then very energetically up but not completely, but slightly bound together with the ribs

6.11   Pulling the bell

6.12   The butterfly seeking a place to sit for a while

6.13 Flying in the air

6.14   The cobra seeking something to eat

6.15   Lifting up the hips and staying on one shoulder and shooting with an arm

6.16   Game with the feet

6.17　　The grass reacting to the wind

6.18   To see behind

6.19   Walking on the spot

6.20   Walk by the water opening with hips

6.21   Running on the spot

6.22   Trying to touch the wall with the hips, with the arms straight, and never touching it

6.23   Stretching the body during the walk

6.24   Playing with the kite

6.25　More actions of the Body Alphabet performed by Giuliano Campo. Opening the chest

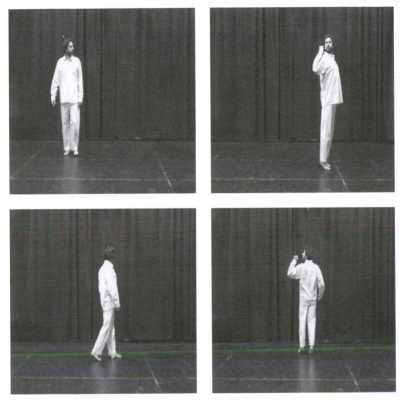

6.26   Walking freely, seeing branches, holding them

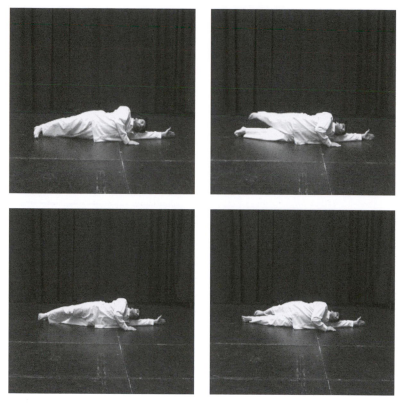

6.27   On the floor. Kicking back

7

SIXTH DAY

The text – Organic and cultural
differences – Voice as a vehicle

Campo: *There must be a reason why we choose to express some thing*
instead of something else. Ethics of aesthetics then, mani-
festing the nature of the choice of the specific form we use for
showing something. I would like to investigate if in your way,
your own poetics, there is a sort of pattern. For me it's clear
that your choices are led by something specific. In all your
steps there is something that continues.

Molik: I would shift your concerns into practical considerations. I
like to work on the texts of Shakespeare. This is what I can
say about poetics. That for me Shakespeare is a great poet,
independently from the fact that he wrote beautiful sonnets.
But besides this he is always a grand poet. So his monologues
are inexhaustible material for actors. For example, I remember
that once when I took *Richard III* I was working with sixteen
people and I told them to choose their monologues from it.
And there were enough monologues for all the girls and all
the boys.

Campo: *But in terms of the conception of the work in your approach*
there is a lot that's going on beyond just the text. Besides, but
even more than the texts that you can choose. Something that
belongs to your life. How can these things work together?

Molik: How do I put them together? Well, practically speaking, during
the training we also have some time to seek the Life. After fifteen,
twenty minutes of warming up we have free time when everybody
starts looking for the Life. Something important happens when
someone finds the interesting Life. Interesting Life for me is the
so-called 'encounter with the unknown'. So during the training
he finds a partner who appears to him in the space, somewhere by
the wall, for example. And he stays for three, four minutes with
this imaginary partner who in this moment is becoming a real

partner. Then his actions are very real, very alive, his reactions and his actions are very real and in this moment the real Life of the body is being created. And when I see it in this moment, I ask him later to come back to it, to return to that moment and try to reconstruct it. And with my help it normally goes on, it goes well. He can reconstruct these three minutes of the training when he found this encounter with this partner who appeared to him. It's not always necessary that there is a partner there, but it is this moment; he has found this moment of his past life and he has just reacted to it as it was a new life. In this moment he could dream, he could have a reverie of that life, or he could just have a sort of *souvenir* of that, a remembrance of something. And then we just take this moment, or these few moments, and then I either first ask him to sing out this Life, to improvise a song of this Life, or, if it is very clear, obvious, evident, I immediately ask him to try to say his text with that Life, immediately, without passing through the step of singing it. And in such a way the first version of the first structure for the monologue is formed. Sometimes his Life and his text go very well together, but sometimes the Life is far away from the text. Apparently far away, but as a matter of fact, even if at first it seems that it isn't possible to put it together with the text, after some time it fits very well. So we have this interesting moment of seeking the unknown. The meeting with the unknown, during the training. And later it shifts to become the structure for the monologue through the individual work. It easily happens that a given person doesn't follow the meaning of the text but follows this Life that was found in the training, with this meeting with the unknown. And on this, with that Life, he says the monologue. So of course he must realise that the text must be clear, must be well articulated and so on, but its logic doesn't come from the text but from the Life. From his personal Life, which could eventually be, and very often is, far away from the text. However, it fits together well with the text.

Campo: *But their choice can't be casual. The text and the Life need some links for being true in the expression.*

Molik: No. Not at all.

Campo: *So they can be casually connected?*

Molik: This Life can be quite strange to the text.

Campo: *Let me say that I have even seen some of the greatest actors of our epoch just using any text, and then exercising something physically, creating somehow some forms, and then putting them together. Or the other way round. It can work for the spectator, but there is still something a bit strange there, not really organic, I may say.*

Molik: Yes, I know what you mean, but my work isn't like that. What you are talking about now are just some kinds of experiment that you can do. You can do anything with movements and words, you can just put something on physical actions, for example, like reciting numbers, telephone numbers, whatever. My work is quite different; no, it's not like that. Because the Life in this case is very real. Because someone has found it, and he has really lived it. And later he has sung it. Expressing this Life in his or her song. And later it changes, he or she replaces this sound with text. He now articulates the sound into the words of the monologue.

Campo: *So in such a way the text is embodied. After all, I can see that there is a link on the level of the meaning, even if it is not that explicit. He connects the truth of the Life with a kind of universal truth expressed by the monologues that you choose, like the Shakespearian monologues. Then the monologues must be carefully chosen.*

Molik: Yes, of course.

Campo: *This is very important, because there are lots of misunderstandings about the work on physical actions, like for example about what Meyerhold used to do, working with different parts of the expressions and putting them together through a montage. The point is that there must be links, even if they are not evident or they don't use the communal logic. Otherwise it's just a formalistic exercise, it can work for the spectator but not for the self.*

Molik: Yes. And it isn't this.

Campo: *This makes me wonder about the truth and the essence of theatre. Is it one and the same thing?*

Molik: Not really. There are different kinds of truths, and the essence is one only.

Campo: *This is a very interesting consideration.*

Molik: Everybody has wide margins to think about what I said.

Campo: *It sounds like a* koan, *the Zen Buddhist philosophical compositions. Something that pushes you to think about the thing. You don't get an answer from a* koan, *you just have to think about it.*

Molik: Exactly. These kinds of expressions function better for the participants. Because they're not like walled in, but everything is open there. It's funny that sometimes it works very well that I say something that I know very well they cannot understand. I just leave it there. I open a door in front of them and that's all. And I don't also know which doors, of course.

Campo: *Now another three words come to mind: simplicity, complexity or easiness, something easy. It's often hard to see the difference between something simple and something easy. Or even between something simple and something complex. It's difficult to be aware of the differences and the similarities, but this is essential for the work on the self.*

Molik: Everything is complex. Even simplicity is complex. Easy is less complex, but as you know, sometimes it is very difficult to do something easy. And it can happen the other way round as well, that sometimes something difficult is very easy. Anyway the preponderance is on the word complexity. That all is complexity. Everything is complex.

Campo: *But the expression must be simple or complex?*

Molik: The expression should be simple. But how to do it when the affair is complex and how to express it simply, that is always the question. And the question is in this term: complex.

Campo: *So obstacles are useful for creativity.*

Molik: Of course, because if everything is easy, quite easy, then normally the result is nothing, everything is flat. And instead, if you have to seek the solution of the problem, if you must fight for victory, then everything gets its value. Because normally nothing that is easy has a value in our language. I mean, in this domain in which we are now. Think of the film *Dyrygent* set in Brzezinka.

Campo: *Yes, there are many interesting and beautiful images and sounds, especially around the end, although on the whole nothing is very clear.*

Molik: Of course not, because the illustration of the process of work is quite confused. But I mean that there you can see what you can achieve in five days, these beautiful four minutes of singing at the end. What clarity, what clear voices, what a beautiful chorus, and that was only thanks to them and their work. Because about the rest, all you can see is just po-po-po, moving the arms around and so on. There was nothing special beside that, just oriented efforts. But in the last four minutes something very special happened.

Campo: *I want to ask you something about emotions. How is it possible to work with the emotions? It's very well known in our domain that the emotions can't be controlled. Nevertheless they are very important, essential, so what is a good way to work with the emotions?*

Molik: How can you say that they cannot be controlled? Emotions have to be controlled. Because otherwise you could kill a partner on stage. They must be controlled. Otherwise there would be many dead men in the theatre.

Campo: *I know that it is possible to control the behaviour, as the original Stanislavski texts taught all of us. I still wonder if it is possible to control the emotions without losing them. I can say, for example, following your provocation: 'I want to kill you', and by controlling the behaviour I stop myself because I know that I cannot actually do it. But a genuine psychological impulse must come from myself in order to perform a credible action. I need to switch on the impulse of 'I want to kill you' and then another physical impulse should come from another part of myself, a controlling mind, just to oppose the consequence of the previous one. In that way it can be controlled.*

Molik: It must be controlled. It is different. It is rather a question of how to provoke the emotions to full life and not to lose control of them. That is the question. Not the other, of how they can be controlled. The question is how to evoke the real emotions and not to lose control, and not to fall into madness.

Campo: *Yes, I understand, and although art can be used to fight illnesses like madness, history is full of sad examples of performers who lost the battle, like Antonin Artaud. This work on the control of the self makes me think of some masters who didn't come from the theatre but from other fields, masters of human beings, like Sulerzhitsky, Stanislavski's great friend and collaborator, or Gurdjieff. Grotowski was in some ways very close to Gurdjieff, even if, of course, he couldn't meet him. Did he ever talk to you about Gurdjieff and his conception of intelligence, soul, emotions and control, or was it just something that he was studying, that he was working on for his own interest?*

Molik: It's a kind of exaggeration to say that Grotowski was very close to Gurdjieff. No, he just knew some stories, his biography and so on, but nothing special, no.

Campo: *I would like to go back to the issues of repetition and its consequence of becoming mechanical. There's always the risk of being mechanical when you repeat the same score too much, which on the other hand is indispensable for achieving the necessary precision. But the risk is that you lose the Life.*

97

So the question is, how to keep the Life every time you repeat the action, in other words, how to become able to improvise within a precise score. I wonder if in your practice you use something specific for it, or if you and Grotowski had thought of using something like a psychological tool for this purpose during the performances and the rehearsals. I remember that you said that every time you performed was different because, for example, the weather was different, the place was different, and so it could never be the same. But what I would like to know is if still, in the moment of the performance, you could use some tricks, some strategies for keeping yourselves alive when you felt that the Life was going away. I would like to know if you have ever used these kinds of psychological instruments, anything. For example, I know that Stanislavski used to try different ways for maintaining it, some exercises, some kinds of tricks for the actor. For example, something that Stanislavski used to ask in case an actor was losing the Life was something like concentrating on a specific detail while he was performing the action.

Molik: Of course, this way can also be tried. But I can tell you that ultimately there is no instrument to use in that case. You must just fight for this Life, for this your own Life that you are losing. Using everything, the whole energy. You know that you must stay alive. You must fight and fight. And that is all that you can do. There are no other means.

Campo: *I remember now a conversation I had with a performer who comes from this tradition. She said that if you are losing the Life you just have to work more with your score, going deeper inside your score.*

Molik: Of course, you must follow your path. In other words you must go into your score. Yes, it is the same concept; you must follow your path and not worry about it. In other words, you must survive it.

Campo: *Another interesting issue is the material condition of art, how the material condition can affect your own work and art. For example, what are the consequences in the work of the differences between places and people, like how different is working or performing in England or in Italy or in France or working with people coming from Poland or Russia or from other countries of Eastern Europe? We already talked about different human races, but I mean people just coming from different countries, from different cultures, even if they belong* to the same race. Which means that we cannot find an organic difference in that sense, because we handle people with similar physical structure, but we face a cultural difference instead. This also involves our relationship with the spectators. I have found differences performing and teaching in different countries. The question for me is to understand specifically how this affects the work, and in what way.

Molik: Oh God, you pose a crucial question, which is how to adapt in different contexts or different people's cultures. How can I know it now? I have no idea now. But I can tell you practically, from my experience, that in a given moment I am sure that I would know what to do and to say. But now I can't answer the question because I'm not in the situation. The matter is that the work is always organic and any situation requires a proper action and reaction. I remember that once I had an Indian boy. I already told you briefly about him. It was a group just near Berlin in which there was an Indian boy. And his voice was very specific, because the Indian voice is different from the European voice. However, I wanted to improve it. So we did some exercises in order to improve it; not to change it, but to make this very specific voice that he had more open. And this was possible, but it took a few days before we reached the point. It took a certain time. Because his voice was not big enough, it was too small, independently from the fact that it was a different kind of voice compared to the European voice. However, it was possible to make it more open, and quite simply bigger. And better at the same time.

Campo: Do you think in Europe the type of voice is homogeneous, or there are some differences between countries and cultures?

Molik: No, it is more or less the same. There are no remarkable differences between France, England, Germany, etc; it is more or less the same *apparatus*. So we can say the differences are just local. They are not basic differences.

Campo: Not organic.

Molik: Not organic, yes, that's right.

Campo: And so generally speaking the white North Americans are the same too.

Molik: The same, yes. But for example, with the Chinese and the Japanese voice there is an organic difference.

Campo: So the culture doesn't affect this work too much. The point is always the organic system.

Molik: Culture doesn't affect, but it makes differences. So the approach must be different. As I told you with the example of this Indian boy, I had to deal with his voice using another approach.

Campo: *But maybe with the Indian boy you found also an organic difference. How is your approach different, for example, with an Italian and with a German?*

Molik: Yes, the Indian voice is also organically different, but between Italians and Germans, no, with these there are no organic differences and so no different approaches are required. And for them the culture does not make any difference. But for example, with Dutch people I had some problems, as I told you, because they have a very special manner of speaking. However, the difference wasn't organic. It was just cultural. It was rather the way they were used to speaking. But when we came to the text, already at the work on the text, they could say it properly. Their larynxes and their mouths were opened normally and the stream of the sound went fluently, came out fluently, without this 'cho-cho-cha-cho-cho-cha', their very specific endemic pronunciation.

Campo: *What in theatre is the relationship between theory and practice? For example, what role does the knowledge of history have?*

Molik: The theory gives some general knowledge, yes. But the practice is a quite different thing. So, you can be a very good theoretician and know very little about the practice. But in theory you can know everything. All systems, all methods and so on. But how they work practically is quite another thing, it's quite different. And on the contrary, you can be a great actor and you can have no idea about the rules, about the methods, about anything. And you can be a genius actor. So they do not go well together anyway. Either you are a very good theoretician or you are an animal, and then you are a good actor.

Campo: *That could be the role of the director, which is a quite contemporary role, at least in our sort of institutional form, since probably the function always existed, although in a different form. In a way, the director must be this connection. I'm thinking of the example of Eisenstein, who was a great theoretician and a great director, and he was even an actor at the beginning. And of course Stanislavski, who was a performer and also someone who worked having a clear view, a strong cognition of the work. So in a way the director can constitute this connection.*

Molik: Yes, but I do not think he was an outstanding actor. Because he was outstanding in a different field of theatre. So it happens that an actor, someone who wants to be an actor, becomes an outstanding man of the theatre. For example Grotowski was like this. He was also an actor. His formation was first as an actor. And he even tried to play something. But he wasn't born to it. He was born for something else.

Campo: But you haven't seen him playing. He never performed anything since you met him.

Molik: No. But I can imagine. It would be funny.

Campo: After all he used to say that directors, like himself, cannot be good actors. And also that the actors should not be too intelligent. That a director is usually someone not so good as an actor and so he becomes a director. He used to say it, probably thinking of his own experience.

Molik: Probably, yes.

Campo: In terms of practical knowledge then, when you work for opening different people's voices, you have to work with different parts of the organism, so always my question is whether you have a very clear and general notion of these centres where you work exactly, rather than experiencing with each individual in a different way, and whether you can say that you have individuated these centres through your personal experiences. I already asked you if you have discovered a universal structure of centres of energies in the human body where you concentrate your work on and through the voice. You said you don't want to tell, but you know it, you built your own diagram. The question I didn't ask yet is why you don't want to talk about it.

Molik: Because I see no need for that. At any time I could explain that I do something for this reason, for that reason or for that other reason. But I don't want to disperse the attention. I say what is necessary to say and I omit what is not necessary to say. Anyway it isn't like I'm always sure, that for me everything is clear. Because I try to guess. I try out this way or that way. And first I must be sure whether it works or not. So very often it's like searching in the dark. It isn't like I always know exactly what I have to do and I am going to do with any person.

Campo: But you follow a pattern, like trying this and this and this. Or is it total improvisation?

Molik: No, it is total improvisation. I know that every time there must be a specific point and an effective way, but I don't know them. It's my guess. Very often.

Campo: So you can't say that there are some points that work every time.

Molik: Actually there are some points that work every time. But besides this there are many surprises, because everything is very individual. Every person is a very individual case, so to speak. So very often I guess. And if it works, if I see that it's alright, that we are on a good road, then we continue. And if not, I try again, I give another proposal, and we follow another way. Sometimes I guess well the first time. But sometimes it works the second time or the third time. And sometimes it takes a few minutes before I get to the point. It works like that. I'm like a doctor who has a patient and must find out what's the illness. Sometimes it's clear at once. But sometimes what is wrong with him must be searched for. What point is not right and there is something wrong. Then you must get to it. It's simple, it's very normal.

Campo: What kinds of problems do you usually see, do you find?

Molik: Usually it's the not-open larynx, or bad breathing, not the right way of breathing. And these are the main two points: not-open larynx, and bad breathing. For example, the breath is taken in the wrong way, as if one had a stopper, is plugged up and is blocked and the person can just give something like a 'hech!' Then first you must work on the breath. And only later do I try to open the sound, to find the voice. This is how it goes.

Campo: It's like removing a cork, like opening a bottle.

Molik: Yes, it's doing the right thing for taking the breath, for not closing the larynx afterwards, for not putting the cork into it.

Campo: So to make the air circulate all the time in the whole organism.

Molik: Yes, and very often when someone takes the breath without the body but just with the mouth, he gives this 'hech!' because it's plugged in the upper part of the chest. And then he vocalises 'Ahh' with a blocked voice. So we must change the breath, so that he doesn't take it just with the lungs, but with the whole body. With the middle part, with the pelvis, with the diaphragm, from down to up. Not from up to down. It happens very often that bad breathing, a wrong way of breathing, enables good singing, or even quite simply speaking. It can't operate in a right way with the voice, with the sound.

Campo: And about the speech, do you only give indications concerning the way the organism functions, or do you think that the attention on respiration should be concentrated more on some *specific elements of the words? There are some interesting old systems used by great actors and teachers like Louis Jouvet,[1] for instance, who used to talk about the differences between vowels and consonants when you speak, suggesting to pay attention only to the first. And of course, it can be experimented the other way around, depending on what you're looking for.*

Molik: It depends, yes. When someone has problems with the closed larynx, then I must pay attention to opening the larynx. If someone takes his breath in such a wrong way that it makes free singing or a free speaking impossible, then I must pay attention to that. These are basic things to do in order to have the breath and the voice open. But yes, I understand what you mean by the example you gave. If there is a specific case, then I must make a specific intervention in order to cancel this problem, to improve someone's skills. Very often it happens that someone is concentrating more on the consonants. And he can't keep the mouth and the larynx free. Then of course there is a problem. So we must seek the way to solve it. And that's quite simple.

Campo: *I would like to talk about something else now. The concept of verticality.*

Molik: This is a very specific concept of Grotowski. I used it many years ago, and Grotowski later used the word 'vehicle'[2] for that kind of energy utilised for verticality. But I also used the term 'vehicle' years before him, in order to explain the role of voice in the human organism, that it's like a vehicle which brings out the whole Life. So, not only the sound, not only the breath, but also the soul. That voice for me was this kind of vehicle. And it depends whether it's vertical or not, because when I'm lying horizontally it's not vertical, but it goes in the direction of the level of the floor. However, it goes vertically in relation to my body. Because it goes always from down to up, from the base of the spine, up to the head, or even to the breast, depending on what resonators you use later, where the sound concentrates. But the sound is always born out from the base of the spine, should be born around the base of the vertebral column. That is always the source of the sound. However, it's important that first it should come from the earth. Very often you take the power from the earth. By the feet, by the legs, by the lower part of the legs, by the upper parts of the leg, by the hips, and then you give yourself the energy to create the sound and it starts somewhere. Very often it's taken directly from the base of the spine and then it goes by different resonators and then you can shape it, you can make it soft, or you can make it very strong. If you add the resonators of the chest you can get different colours of the sound made with the voice. But if you go higher, in *la nuque*, the nape of the neck, you have this very sharp sound, very high. And also by the upper part of the head, from the forehead. But I try to never use the head for speaking or for singing. As I said, for me the highest point is *la nuque*. And of course, if you want to formulate words you have to use your mouth. This is quite obvious. It's natural that when you speak, you ultimately speak with the mouth. With your tongue, with your mouth, with your teeth. But this is only when you give the sound, the voice, its final shape.

Campo: *I was thinking of the Chinese practitioners. They always inspire me, especially when they talk about breathing the energy. They also say that they take the energy from the earth, but they say they take it also from the sky, from the top of the head. It's like breathing continuously up and down, and not just from down to up.*

Molik: Yes, but I think that it belongs to their culture. From how and where they speak from. They speak quite differently from European people. They use and modulate all high tunes from the head, they speak like this: 'Hi-ho-chu-ya-kah-hi-koh-iah-khon-kinh-kih.' So this is now another problem, a problem of culture.

Campo: *About the Process again. How was it discovered? When and how did it happen? Was there a project for experimenting with it, a specific research passing through many attempts, or was it just discovered during your practice?*

Molik: The Process started from the very beginning of the world.

Campo: *So it always happened, since the very beginning of the company.*

Molik: No, not the very beginning of the company, but the beginning of the world. Without the Process there would be no civilisation, no humanity maybe, there would be nothing. I see that you are amazed.

Campo: *Yes, I am amazed, because I'm thinking of something very specific.*

Molik: Yes, I know. You mean the kind of Process in the actor's world.

Campo: *Yes. You said that at a certain moment you started to use, to work, in Process. You experimented with the Organic Process. In fact that was a definition that Grotowski used to give. The Process in your work, as a specific term, was indicating a different level of consciousness, or trance. A sort of alteration in the consciousness in the work.*

Molik: It is a fact that such a thing exists. The Process in the actor's work is a research, and probably in any work it exists. Every work starts probably from the process of research. So the Process is that you start something and you develop it, and then you achieve it, you reach your aim or not. This is the Process. You explore something, you are searching, you are doing your own research, your quest in the unknown. Very often this Process is this seeking in the unknown. The Process has many aspects. It's something that starts and then evolves and reaches the point or not. And sometimes this Process is the most interesting element of the work and it is more important than the result. We can have a long digression on this theme, but this isn't the moment for it. The beginning of the Process in our work very often was, and is, absolutely unconscious. You don't know where it comes from. And that Process, that certain, specific Process starts. And then you must just follow it as long as it is possible, until the Process just stops. And it is cut and doesn't exist any more. But a little later, a few minutes later, or a few days later, or even a few weeks later, it's also possible to try to find how to follow up on this 'work in Process'.

Campo: *Working for recalling it.*

Molik: To recall it and to continue. And finding how to follow up on this. Yes, *la suite. Trouver la suite.*

Campo: *Do you think that all actors work somehow in a sort of Process, or that it was or it is something very specific for some occasions and some kinds of work?*

Molik: I can't say much about it, just because I don't know everyone, and how everybody tries to realise his own dreams and his own desires. Because normally the Process is an expression of dreams or realisation of some desires which are important for yourself, something that has the greatest importance for yourself. It's what you want to reach. And it depends on everyone's life experiences, so I cannot say anything about how it goes for others. Anyway, the Process is an action. But it's an action which rarely comes out on the surface of our life, so there the point is how to get it on the surface of our life. How to materialise this Process in order to have an effect, to reach the point, to reach certain goals. Because the Process is very often only partly conscious, and very often it's unconscious. So very often you are losing the concept of what to do, how to follow this Process and when is the time to stop it. And how long you can follow it, that is always the question. That is the Process. It's always something *in statu nascendi*. Being during the time. So it is very complex. You can't easily find the definition of what it is exactly.

Campo: *Do you think that at times it can be dangerous for the organism?*

Molik: Often yes. Maybe not very often, but let me say that sometimes it can be very dangerous. And anyway, it is always more or less dangerous. Because you never know where your Process will lead you, where you are going to.

Campo: *Do you think that this has affected the health of some members of the company?*

Molik: This I don't know because I don't feel affected by it. But some of the members, maybe yes, have been affected a little bit by it. Because very often this experience makes you very dizzy, like what you have on the brink of a great danger. And the rest depends on the personal constitution. My constitution was rather resistant to such danger, fortunately.

Campo: *Now to other topics. Balance. The importance of balance, and so work on balance, and on which kind of balance. And also if there is a specific balance for the voice. One of the principles of Theatre Anthropology is that the performers work with a different kind of balance, which is not the balance of the everyday life but is a sort of luxurious balance, as Barba says. Because we do something different from everyday life and we move towards and around the extreme points, with an exceptional expenditure of energy unimaginable in everyday life. This is what the theatre anthropologists study. So I wonder if there is a sort of balance also for the voice. If you work on the balance of the voice as well as of the body.*

Molik: The definition of balance is very broad. There is the physical, the body balance. But there are also other different kinds of balances. The most important is between physics and psyche. Of course you must keep always the balance of the voice too, otherwise you could do very strange things! I remember for example a group of people who were looking for the baby's

106

first cry at birth. It was called something like the technique of the First Cry. It was such a technique that is intended to provoke your first 'Uaahh!' Years ago I took part in a group which tried such a thing; I found it very damaging and very dangerous. It lacked balance. There was no balance in it, there was just the idea of pushing towards the extreme. And just doing extreme things with the voice, what's it for? No, such a thing should never take place. So the work on the balance of voice is that you invite someone to give the maximum of himself on the level of the vibration of the sound, but never force the voice. Never. It is possible to touch the impossible with a sound which is pure vibration, without a high voice, without a strong voice. And this is important, so we can say that balance is very important in that area of the activity, that is, to try to find the balance between the power of vibration and the sound. That the voice should never be dominating in the sound, but rather the vibration should be, if something is to be dominating. And usually there should be a balance between the sound, the voice and the vibration. Very often there is a fault, an error, which is abusing the voice. On work on voice, the most common mistake is abusing it.

Campo: *About vibrations. Of course there are different vibrations, different kinds of vibrations. Maybe the difference is in terms of rhythm; I mean, physically, the wave is different.*

Molik: Probably, yes.

Campo: *But do you not think that there is one specific vibration for each individual, like one single specific sound that is the perfect sound, the true sound of an individual?*

Molik: As I said, it's very easy to check it. Physically. When you are in the room, you hear your sound, which is pure vibration, and at the same time you can hear three or four sounds, three or four notes of your own sound. I don't use the word voice because here there's more sound than voice. When it's almost pure vibration you hear exactly three or four notes. Because you have such a clear resonance that a sound divides into three or four tones, three or four notes. So it's easy to check when you open the voice, listening to the open sound and hearing the pure vibration, and when instead it's just voice or the mixture of voice and sound. When you give just voice, then you can hear only one resonance, and two when there is this mixture.

Campo: *I came back to this point because I was wondering about some traditions, especially religious, like the Vedic, and also*

107

some Christian Orthodox traditions, that at certain advanced stages of personal training, or practice of praying, try to find the true sound of the individual, as if there was one, to coincide with a more complex unique vibration of the universal spirit. Of course the aim of such an effort is in the end to reach the universal sound, the mystic source of the world for the Vedic tradition, that is the Logos for the Christians, as indicated by St John at the beginning of his gospel.

Molik: Everyone has his own voice. The most important thing is to have your own voice, yes. Not to try to do it this way or that way, for example vocalising 'Eh-eh' with a low tone, or 'Ah-Ah' with a high tone, or something like this. But just try to have your natural voice. This is one thing. And later another problem is what you can do with this. Because you can just speak without any vibration, flat, mumbling something like 'que-que-que' or you can make it vibrate more, giving a more open and sounding voice, like 'boh-boh-boh'. It depends on the circumstances in which you are speaking. It depends on the situation, too.

Campo: *The concept sounds very similar, because this search for your own voice is probably also a way to find your true sound, or vibration, or most probably the range of vibrations which are maybe unknown to yourself and that you have to discover.*

Molik: Of course, but very often it depends on the circumstances. And that is all.

8

SEVENTH DAY

The attention – Necessity, Organic Process, nostalgia

Campo: *Attention.*

Molik: Attention. The word's like a bell. Like a big bell: 'attention please', yes! It's something that most often is innate. You come, you appear in the world with attention or without attention, and then you go through all your life like that, being attentive or not attentive. There are different kinds of attention. Attention can be for the self, and also for others. As you know, attention on yourself isn't so good, because if someone has too much attention on himself he's not well regarded. Do you agree?

Campo: *Yes, I understand. Now we are talking about caring, like taking care or taking something as important. I think something is important so I pay attention to it. But there's another kind of attention that's very important in the work. You can think of the attention itself, and as you told me once, this kind of process of attention is something like taking something from the external and then working with that internally, and then giving it back to the external. For example, for Simone Weil,[1] the attention itself is the vehicle. Her concept of highest attention is very similar to the 'highest connection', using Grotowski's late terminology. I remember Grotowski used to talk about attention, in some important but still unpublished lessons he gave at the University of Rome in 1982, referring to a 'colleague' coming from a distant culture, a Mexican Huichol. This 'performer' (in a Grotowskian sense[2]) was trying to explain in another language what he was doing and what it was important to do in such a specific activity, and the translation was basically 'being attentive', having 'the feet well placed on the ground'.*

Molik: If you're looking for the unknown, if you're seeking the meeting with the unknown, as the material for building the structure for a monologue, yes, you must be very attentive, but you must be relaxed, and then you do nothing. And since you are relaxed and then you do nothing you easily risk losing attention. In fact, what do you do in that moment? Actually you do nothing. However, you must be very attentive, because even the smallest element that you find can pull your attention and then create the rest. From this smallest point it gets bigger and bigger, you see it growing, growing, and then finally you see the real partner coming, and then you have now the Life between you and the partner, who is in front of you, who doesn't exist in reality, but for you it is a real partner. And in that context yes, being attentive is very important. Just because you are relaxed, like a butterfly for example, as we do very often, when I say: 'let's be butterflies now'. And then, in this very moment something unexpected suddenly happens, and a whole other world is standing in front of your eyes, and you see the new Life, another new place, another time. You find yourself in a quite different place, like somewhere you are very often in your dreams, when you're lying in bed but you dream that you're in a wonderful orchard or in a wonderful landscape somewhere, where looking far away you see beautiful landscapes, maybe somewhere that you feel as if you have the wind in your face. But everything can change in a second. For two or three minutes you find a new Life, which you can use later, with the text for example, once it's already found and reconstructed. So, in such a moment the attention is very important so that you don't lose this moment. Because it's like 'puit', a fraction of a second. You catch it or not. The funny thing is that you can't do this kind of research consciously. It doesn't work like this, that you're in the room and you are thinking of how to find the meeting with the unknown and you decide to start now, seeking for the meeting with the unknown. No, in that way, in that manner, nothing can be possible. It must come from the existing Life, when the reality changes, after around fifteen minutes, when very slowly the reality changes. At first we start from the training. And then there is mixture, mixture, mixture. There are so many people here, twelve people or fifteen people, and then there are some short meetings between one and another and there is one point, there is one corner over there, and in a certain moment something stops you, and then this unknown appears, realised. It appears to you and it's getting real. And then also your physical behaviour is changing completely. And then you are

already in another place and in another time. And you have
these just two minutes in which you live another Life. You're
no longer in this room where you are working, but you're in
your personal environment, something that's very personal to
you, where you have this very special meeting. Then everything is changing. You forget that you're in the room, because
you have other problems, another physical sensation. It makes
you do a gesture that you have no idea what it is. However,
the funny thing is that later you'll remember. After these two
minutes you come back to the normal training and then, when
the training's over, you remember. You remember that you
have had such a meeting with the unknown. And that it was
interesting and it was important for you. In such a way you
have found a structure for the Life to use for the monologue,
for instance. And then you have the monologue, which is built
on the personal Life, which is found in such circumstances
during the training. Because if you don't have such a thing,
how can you build a monologue? Only by the imagination
which comes out of the text, from the words, from the text
itself? This isn't so very interesting. I wonder how all this will
look on paper, once you put my words on paper and someone
will read them. I just ask myself the question whether it is
possible to understand it or not, if it will sound just abstract.
It's a question. Nobody knows.

Campo: *It is a very old problem. An ancient problem I might say;
language and communication and the form of transmission.
Most of the ancient masters, for instance, used to refuse
writing, like Socrates, who was transcribed by Plato, or the
ancient Indian saints who didn't want to transcribe the Veda.
The immense corpus of scriptures we have of the Veda now is
just a small part of what has been orally transmitted for thousands of years, and in a way, Grotowski is like this too. They
just refused to write and were often against writing.*

Molik: Yes, it's an eternal question. Better not to worry too much.

Campo: *What about vanity?*

Molik: *Vanitas vanitatum et omnia vanitas.* I was never interested in
vanity, because I never had such a problem. Or even such a
temptation. So I don't know what vanity is.

Campo: *Maybe this is valid for yourself, but what about others? For
example Louis Jouvet, who was also a great teacher, and so
used to meet many students of acting, used to say that normally
actors start from vanity. Then, if they work correctly, going*

deeply through the profession and the work of the actor itself,
they discover that it functions in the opposite way. But very
often vanity is the first impulse, the first reason why someone
wants to be an actor.

Molik: Yes, probably it could be like that. But concerning myself, no, I started to be an actor from modesty, not from vanity. So I can't say anything about this topic. It's absolutely strange for me.

Campo: *But you must see students, pupils, actors, having this charac-teristic.*

Molik: When it is too evident I say something. But when it's on a normal level I never pay any attention to it. Because it's human, everything is human. And also, a little bit of vanity isn't a bad thing, as you know.

Campo: *Now, going to the opposite of the so-called 'ego': what is the 'total act'? What was the 'total act'?*

Molik: You must have read something about it.

Campo: *I know the texts. I've read* Towards a Poor Theatre, *many times.*

Molik: So, if you know it, why are you asking?

Campo: *Because of lack of real experience. My generation never had a clear idea of it. We can see the films or read the texts but we don't have, we never had, any concrete experience of it.*

Molik: Ah-ah, you never experienced such a thing as the total act? Well, the total act is what happens when you're giving yourself absolutely into something. It happens when you forget about yourself totally and you're only the spirit that is giving the act that you are doing in a given moment. When you forget everything else, when you don't remember anything else but this moment in which you are. Then, in this moment, there is the 'total act'.

Campo: *It's known as a special definition given to Cieślak's work for* The Constant Prince.

Molik: Yes.

Campo: *But you experienced it as well.*

Molik: Yes, it happened. It happened a few times, so I know it also from my personal experience.

Campo: *Was it on stage, in some specific productions?*

Molik: Yes. There were moments. Not so many, really, to tell the truth. But there were some.

Campo: *Was it at the time of* The Constant Prince?

Molik: No, it wasn't possible in *The Constant Prince*. It happened in *Akropolis*.

Campo: *I was thinking of* Akropolis *and its musical complexity. Do you think it's important for an actor to be able to play instruments and to study music?*

Molik: I think so. It's not that important but it is very helpful, anyway. It is very helpful to play a little bit of anything.

Campo: *I was thinking about the difference between professionals and amateurs.*

Molik: It depends from which angle you're looking at it. The word *amateur* comes from *amor, amare*. So it is a lot, but it's not enough. Professional is someone who from this *amor, amare*, became professional. I mean that starting from the love of the thing, he makes it professional. On the level of basic differences it's just like this and nothing else. *Amateur* is the beginner; professional is someone who now has much more experience. Every professional was first amateur, but then step by step became a professional. The only difference is on the level of experience, I believe.

Campo: *What do you think about the amateur theatre, or unprofessional people who just do it, who just meet and practise theatre together.*

Molik: I like the idea of amateur theatre. There are fewer and fewer experiences now of these kinds of amateur theatres, at least in Poland. Once upon a time there were many amateur theatres, in every town, in every small town, even in the countryside. But now, less and less. It's a pity.

Campo: *Do you ever have amateurs participating in your workshops?*

Molik: Very often.

Campo: *Often, but normally they're professional.*

Molik: Normally yes, but from time to time there are also amateurs. For example in Berlin it's very usual that some tourists or some elderly ladies or some lawyers, or some teachers come. So, they're not necessarily professional actors, no.

Campo: *Does it make any difference in the work for you, for your approach?*

Molik: My approach is the same for everybody. Whether there's a 17-year-old girl or a very experienced actor it must be the same. They are treated the same as the 17-year-old girl. All the actors for the first days must go through the process of cleaning, of washing. But later I must differentiate between

113

one and the other, since the demands aren't the same for one and for the other. But in the first days the work is the same.

Campo: *What about differences of age?*

Molik: The same. No pity for the elderly people. Actually I don't demand that the elderly people do the same, exactly the same, as the others. I only ask that they find themselves on their level, how they are, and they must join the group well, and that's all. There is no difference. I mean that I don't differentiate between those people who are very experienced, who are good actors, and those who are coming for the first time to do anything with theatre or anything related to it. Because what I am interested in first and foremost is the people. And it's up to them to find their own value and their own demands of themselves, what they want to do. It's up to them, whether someone wants, in the final days, to say just a short poem or a great monologue, very long sometimes. But sometimes some special situations happen, working with teenagers. For example, once in Pula, in Istria, it suddenly happened that I had to run a workshop with 15-, 16-, and 17-year-old girls, and a few boys. So, why not do it? I did a small course. It wasn't real work, not on the organism and so on. I just prepared a few pieces, so that everybody had one song and one small poem. And later it was just academic. On the last day the parents of these kids came and every girl and every boy recited a poem and a song. And it was very simple, it was OK, but it was a sort of academy. Because there was no work on the organism, there was no research into the unknown, which is what I normally do.

Campo: *Because they were too young for it. So you can't work in that way with people who are too young; a minimum age is required for starting the work with this approach.*

Molik: Yes, they were too young, so it happened like this. Yes, there is a minimum age; it is 18. But once it worked with a girl who was 17, but she's been the only one. She was the youngest. The rest of her group were 20, 21 and 23 years old. And she was great, because she had a comprehension of what the others were doing. But I might say that at the end everyone was doing the same thing, so it was not really possible there to have a significant experience.

Campo: *But when someone is old can they still be open? Can he still have the necessary organic flexibility? I find this area of the organic experience through practice of the art particularly interesting. Someone says that an Organic Process can only*

be really experienced before a certain age, like when the
organism is still growing, like until around 35. And then it's
very difficult to experience it, for the first time I mean. If you
don't do it before that age, then it's no longer possible to have
it. But from your experience you say that it is possible.

Molik: Yes. Even at 65. It happened once. I remember in particular
a retired actor who was more than 60, he was around 65, and
two ladies who were about 60, came. And they managed to
do everything like the others, in their own manner of course.
They weren't running, not jumping like the others, but they
were active in their own manner. And it was very good, for
me and for them as well. It was very interesting, yes. They did
it normally, with text, with songs. But I can't say that I know
exactly what an Organic Process is. I can only guess when
an Organic Process is taking place and when it is not. But I
can never be sure. Sometimes it is and sometimes it isn't. You
don't know what's going on. Sometimes it's clear, we see an
Organic Process. Sometimes we say no, this has nothing to do
with an Organic Process. But sometimes I can't say what it is.

Campo: *It's mixed with something else.*

Molik: Yes, it is a kind of mixture.

Campo: *I'm not really surprised about this old actor's skill, but I*
wonder if it is possible with non-professionals.

Molik: Yes, it is possible. In Berlin for example, very often just private
persons come to work, but they still must have one poem and
one song, one text and one song, like everybody else, because
this is the condition. Some have problems with voice, teachers or
lawyers, and the work functions for them. But even ladies who
have nothing to do with any profession came just to try, for the
experience. They had heard about something that is interesting and
they came. And that was good for them. So, in different towns, in
different countries, different things happen. Very often it is exclusively for professionals, but often it's also open for everybody
who wants to come and experience a sort of adventure. Once, for
example, in Barcelona I ran it for academic teachers only, for an
institute of art, and it worked well. There it was done practically
only for the teachers who were interested, and they knew about it
from their students; in fact I'd already been there twice before, but
I'd worked with the students of the school.

Campo: *I'm thinking now of necessity. Which in theatre means that*
you have to do precisely those specific things inscribed in that
precise score or related to that unique character. And you

must survive that condition; you speak that text just because
you have to. But even in our everyday life we're always in a
condition of necessity. We do the things that we have to do. So,
the question is always how to handle it.

Molik: Oh, yes, and everybody does it in his own manner. What it's
necessary to do, has to be done. Then, how to do it, I don't
know. But when it has to be done, it has to be done. And it
is done. 'Where there is need there is need', you know the
saying? Where there is need there is need, where there is need,
you must do it and then it is done. Necessity, necessity. Yes, I
remember a text by Wyspiański, 'konieczność, konieczność'.
In *Akropolis* there was this text, someone was lying on a tube,
and someone else was asking him: 'necessity?' and the other
answered: 'necessity'. So it is when something's obvious.
Quite simply to this question you have this answer: 'Tak,
racja, racja.' [Yes, it is right.]

Campo: *The matter is, how to still be creative or feel free or able to*
search or be alive, when you have to do something.

Molik: When you have to do something you cannot be creative, you
cannot be full of Life; you have to do it.

Campo: *Yes, but this is the point, when having the score, for example,*
the character, the text. You have to do it but you have to be
alive at the same time.

Molik: Of course, but sometimes it's not possible. Even if one is only
one per cent alive, he has to do it. Because necessity is necessity. We had such performances that no one was alive, but
however, we had to do them and we did. What they were like,
God only knows, but we had to do them, so we did. But there
were some performances absolutely without Life between us.

Campo: *Which production was this?*

Molik: *Apocalypsis cum figuris.* There were some performances that
were completely dead.

Campo: *Why?*

Molik: The day, lack of energy, complete lack of contact. It was in
Australia, maybe because of the special climate. No contact,
nothing, completely no energy; we felt terrible afterwards, but
nobody could do anything. We just had an enormous hang-
over.

Campo: *Now, something about nostalgia. Nostalgia as a concept, like*
searching for something original, primitive or natural that's
probably before us. We use the word 'natural' very often for it.
But maybe it's the same as what Rena Mirecka means by 'love'.

She often uses the term 'love'. I wonder if this nostalgia is part of the research or if it's an element in the work. I wonder if this seeking a real Life in the work is a sort of research into a condition that's lost and which probably existed some time before us, that is no longer in the present personal life but is something like an echo of something else. For example, in paratheatre, something that was found through this contact with nature.

Molik: I don't know because I've never experienced such sentiments of nostalgia. But Rena, I believed she had, yes. Me, never. I don't know what it is. I never have time for nostalgia. I'm such a busy man that I never have time for nostalgia. I just like to say: 'ah ma jeunesse, jeunesse … ma jeunesse, jeunesse … '. I repeat it very often: 'nostalgie, c'est nostalgie', yes, but about the rest, I don't have these kinds of reflections. Maybe such a thing exists, but I was really never engaged in paratheatre on this aspect. Yes, I worked a lot with nature, but I don't have any nostalgia for this and I didn't work on it because of nostalgia. It was like any other stage of my life. And yes, this work with nature was very fruitful. I wasn't the same man, not the same actor, before working with nature as I was afterwards. I was much changed. After this contact with nature I was very much renovated, we can say. So it was a very good experience. And that's all.

Campo: *Yes, but when we do this kind of work, why do we do it with nature? I wonder if it's because we're looking for something that we have lost as human beings. Why work with nature, that's the point.*

Molik: This you must ask nature, not me.

Campo: *What is the value of the work on the self? Why work on oneself?*

Molik: I don't know. I never worked on myself, just on the self. I don't know what it is. I always work for somebody or with somebody. I never work on myself for the sake of it.

Campo: *But your pupil, when he or she is doing the activity, is working on himself or herself.*

Molik: Yes he is working on himself.

Campo: *And what's the value of it? Why is it important? What is this for? For which reason is he working?*

Molik: For himself.

Campo: *What is the result of it? Why do it? To be better, to be able to do something, to develop, improve some skills, or for what?*

Molik: Maybe for his own pleasure, I don't know. I don't believe that he'll be better because of it, but I feel that it gives him pleasure. Perhaps it's better to say satisfaction. It gives him satisfaction, so with him I feel useful.

Campo: *There are many other ways of getting pleasure; this is a very specific, special kind of activity.*

Molik: This is one of them, so I have chosen this one.

Campo: *Do you think that there should be pleasure in acting, in theatre?*

Molik: No, I don't think that we're talking about acting and theatre now. Now we're speaking about people.

Campo: *Yes, but it still makes me think about it. There are some scholars now who believe that in theatre there must be pleasure. I'm not sure about it. Frankly, I find this problematic because the pleasure is always directed to the satisfaction of the self, of the so-called 'ego' I might say. So I find this idea particularly dangerous when applied to theatre. It would be a serious problem, since all the work is directed to getting beyond the ego, and this is the inner sense of the 'total act'. That's why I prefer to use the term 'joy' instead of 'pleasure' to indicate the final aim of the theatre, our highest achievement. Simone Weil, again, used to say that pleasures are always negative. I don't know if it's correct or not, so I wonder. This is another matter anyway. Here we can talk about pleasure in acting, if there must be pleasure in theatre or not, and how, when, in which aspect of it, in which way. I don't know if this is right at all.*

Molik: Neither do I know.

Campo: *Did you ever experience pleasure in acting?*

Molik: In fact not so much in acting, but in this lifestyle, yes. I find a kind of pleasure in it, and anyway if it's not real pleasure, I may say that I like this style of life. Which is very often very difficult, and I find the pleasure right in these difficulties, in fighting these difficulties. Maybe this is a sort of compensation for not being a warrior, it's a kind of substitute.

Campo: *That could be the nostalgia of not being a warrior.*

Molik: Yes, in this sense we're not far from nostalgia. So we come back to the point at the beginning.

Campo: *I'd like to know something more about paratheatre and the beginning of it. How was the beginning of paratheatre for you, and what actually happened?*

Molik: The beginning of paratheatre, this period, was difficult for me, because at that time I was already a much too professional actor.

118

The others in the group were more or less open, because they were not as professional as me. So I had some problems. So at the beginning, as you remember, I was busy with other activities. I was the *chauffeur*, the driver, and I was busy with provisions for the group. Only later I came into the process itself. Only after half a year or so could I take part in these actions in which there were participants, with around thirty or forty or fifty people, and I was one of the leaders, like the others. But at first I was just a little bit aside. I just couldn't find myself in this activity.

Campo: *Did you follow anyone in order to become a leader? Was there someone in a way leading you, training you, or did it come naturally?*

Molik: No, no, at a certain moment I just decided 'I can come in', and I jumped in and I was now OK, I was a natural leader. At once. But at first I kept myself a little aside.

Campo: *I wonder if starting paratheatre was just Grotowski's decision. There wasn't a discussion, an agreement, or communal process. It was just Grotowski's decision.*

Molik: Yes, it was quite simply his idea.

Campo: *And did you agree, all of you, or not? Was there any tension, some discussions?*

Molik: No there was no tension or discussion, but some fitted in at once and others didn't. I was one who could not fit in at once, who needed more time than the others.

Campo: *But the idea was generally accepted.*

Molik: Yes, of course.

Campo: *When I read about paratheatre I always see descriptions of some events, some activities, some actions and some leaders, some guides, but there's never anything really about Grotowski. So what was Grotowski's role in the paratheatre?*

Molik: Well, he got the idea, he gave the idea, and later he was just appearing from time to time. But just for a very short time, just standing by the wall. Yes, he just walked around. He was never taking part in it, he was just the spirit watching everything.

Campo: *He wasn't even involved in the creation of the different actions and projects?*

Molik: No.

Campo: *Was he really just a watcher?*

Molik: He just used to give tasks to everyone. He was organising all this, deciding whether one time it would be for two hours, another time for two days, another time would last one week. He was inventing these events and everything that concerned these activities.

Campo: But what to do practically was just your own business.

Molik: Only ours.

Campo: Something very significant for me is Simone Weil's text at the end of Apocalypsis cum figuris. It's very strange that when I read about Apocalypsis all the other authors, Dostoevsky, Eliot, and the texts from the Bible, are often quoted and there's a lot written about them. But nobody speaks about the text taken from Simone Weil. It is a beautiful, special text.³ It's very important in itself, but also inserted in a crucial position for that production, and for the work of the company in general. It comes at a decisive moment, because it's the last long monologue before the end of the show, to coincide with the end of Grotowski's work on the Theatre of Productions. And yours as well. I wonder if her thinking had any kind of influence in your work, if she was one of the authors you used to read.

Molik: We used not to read her at that time. That was a choice made by Grotowski and Flaszen. They always chose all the texts.

Campo: So they clearly used to read her, it was important for them.

Molik: Yes, she was. The last words, 'Go and never come back', were taken from Dostoevsky, but before there was Simone Weil's text, which we used while washing in the bowls and some other actions related to it.

9

EIGHTH DAY

The productions – Meeting Grotowski – The Teatr Laboratorium

Campo: *Now we can start the second part, commenting on your artistic story. Everything I know was found in different texts, so it is not so easy to reconstruct it with all the details. I made a list of all your performances. We can start by saying a few words, giving just some memories for each one. Maybe the beginning is this* Porwanie Sabinek *in 1957. As far as I know this was your first 'official' production.*

Molik: Yes, it was at the theatre school, in the theatre academy. It was just for the diploma. It's a very nice, very funny play and we did it with great pleasure. Kasimir Rudzki directed this play. It was a comedy.

Campo: *What were you doing?*

Molik: I just played someone's husband.

Campo: *Did you use any particular technique? How did you create the character?*

Molik: No, it was nothing, there was nothing special. It was just a normal school performance.

Campo: *Do you remember any friends, any colleague?*

Molik: Yes, you can see everyone in those pictures,[1] saying goodbye to the theatre school. Some of them were my professors and some were my colleagues. There you can see almost the whole of our class. We started with sixteen but then we lost some people, so when we ended up we were about fourteen. Some I know are still in Warsaw. Some disappeared. In one of the pictures you can see the *accompagnateur* who played the piano when we were singing different songs with Professor Sempolinski, a phenomenal man. He was a big specialist of the *fin de siècle*, and we worked on these songs of the *fin de siècle*: ta-taratta-ta-taratta-ta-tarttatam and so on, pom-pom-pom-pom-pom-pom-pom-pom … these kinds of things. He was a fantastic man. One is Polomski, actually a very well-known *chanteur*, a singer, a kind of Polish Perry Como or something like that, with a very 'confidential', 'easy listening' singing style. And Kasimir Rudzki, who was our Dean, and professors Perzanowska and Witkowski and Bardini, with his moustache. And Lapicki, who at that time was assistant to Rudzki. He was a very young man, 23 maybe, he was almost my age when I finished school. Of course later he became a professor too.

Campo: *Bardini is an Italian name.*

Molik: Probably yes, but he was Polish.

Campo: *Did most of your colleagues have good careers in show business, in theatre or in some related fields?*

Molik: Not really, not so many. Not too many, but however, yes, some of them did. Like Zdzisio Szymborski, who was for a long time at the Theatre Syrena, which has a rather light repertoire. And Wiskowska, who was also there in this theatre, and also Barbara Prosniewska, she was also in the Syrena.

Campo: *Then in 1958 I have different things. In the same year, a couple in Łódź as Komisarz in* Liliomye *('Gangsters'), and as Major in* Pułapce Na Myszy *('The Mousetrap') by Agatha Christie, and another one in Opole, as Maurycy in* Lecie w Nohant. *Can you say anything about these performances?*

Molik: I don't remember exactly what the first ones were. I don't remember what I've done there, but there are some pictures. It was in Łódź, the capital of Polish film, in a theatre called 7.15, Seven and a Quarter. I did them with a friend on the course of my same year. We finished the Theatre Academy at the same time. These were done a year after the end of the Academy. In one I played the doctor, it was a piece by Molnar. Molnar is a Hungarian writer, a playwright. Then in *The Mousetrap*, by Agatha Christie, I played the Major. I had a pipe. He was the elderly man. I was characterised by a beard. And I got the pipe and I smoked the pipe and I was very serious. That's all.

Campo: *Nothing particularly interesting.*

Molik: Nothing really interesting. Then after one year we played *L'été en Nohan* in Opole, a play about Frédéric Chopin. The author was Iwaszkiewicz and Jerzy Antczak was the director. Jerzy Antczak later made a film from the play.

Campo: *What was it? Here you played Maurycy.*

Molik: I was the son of George Sand, of this lady who had a love affair with Chopin. George Sand was with Frédéric Chopin,

Solange was her daughter. And there I played just a young man. It was nothing in particular. Not a big role.

Campo: *Then in 1959, Fabian in a Shakespeare play. What was it exactly?*

Molik: It was *Wieczór Trzech Króli* (*Twelfth Night*). I was one of these three or four characters who just make some jokes.

Campo: *That was the first of your meetings with Shakespeare. So that was interesting for you. It was probably the first really interesting actor's work for you.*

Molik: Yes. It was interesting.

Campo: *What do you remember of that experience?*

Molik: That I wasn't a bad comic at that time. Because I played a comic role there. This I remember – that I wasn't bad as a comic.

Campo: *And then, after that you entered the Teatr Laboratorium. Basically, you founded the company. I mean all together, that was the beginning of the Teatr Laboratorium.*

Molik: Yes. Grotowski found me in the normal theatre, and he came to Opole.

Campo: *You were playing Shakespeare, so you were doing a comic character.*

Molik: Yes but he didn't see me. He remembered me from the theatre school. We met in a summer camp, and we made an appointment.

Campo: *So it was just a personal relationship, not professional. He hadn't seen you on stage.*

Molik: No, never on stage, we just met in the school before.

Campo: *The first production of the Teatr Laboratorium was* Orpheus, *based on Cocteau. How was it?*

Molik: It was an interesting performance. I played this kind of messenger.

Campo: *Can you remember something about it? It is the beginning of the company.*

Molik: I remember that I amazed everyone because at a certain moment I was found just glued to the wall. And for the people it was a huge surprise, because before I was standing on a small *tabouret*, a footstool, by the wall, and my partner came and took the *tabouret* away, and I stayed glued to the wall. Above the *tabouret* there was a piece of iron, so when the *tabouret* was taken away it looked like I was glued. So there was an 'Ahhh' on the part of the spectators, who thought: 'how can he be hanging on the wall, glued?' Just because there was a small piece of metal invisible. And I was standing like this. A big success. I levitated.

Campo: *But how was the work?*

Molik: It was very interesting because the show was made in ten days. Grotowski was completely prepared and he did the whole performance in one week. The whole rehearsal and the preparation, everything in ten days, and the show was ready, and we had the premiere.

Campo: *For how long did you perform it?*

Molik: For three or four weeks. And later there was *Cain*.

Campo: *Yes, in 1960. The year 1960 is full of things.*

Molik: Yes, because every month we did something different.

Campo: *In January there was* Cain. *What style of acting were you using at that time?*

Molik: The scholastic style, which came from the school I'd been at and after that one season in Łódź. So I just did my best and I invented a lot of things. I was very inventive at that time. I was giving suggestions.

Campo: *You had more freedom than afterwards, that's what you mean.*

Molik: Definitely, yes. Later I didn't have as much freedom practically, as in the first performances. At that time I was giving lots of suggestions, and later I was just an executor of Grotowski's ideas. But in the beginning I was always giving many strange ideas that were immediately accepted by Grotowski. All the performances were full of joy. Even if they weren't necessarily comedies, they were very joyful.

Campo: *And this went on until when?*

Molik: It was until 1961, in all these first performances. So in *Orpheus*, in *Cain*, and later also in *Mystery Bouffe*, as well as in *Sakuntala*.

Campo: *Then there's* Forefathers' Eve, *based on Mickiewicz. Were you also having more freedom here, giving ideas?*

Molik: No, not now. Now I was led. This is *Dziady*; in *Dziady* the time that I was always giving full ideas and full innovations was now over. Here I played Konrad, a big national hero.

Campo: *There was a change. So this is the moment of change.*

Molik: Yes, this was the change.

Campo: *I see that there are other things in 1961. You were actor-director in* Pamiętnik, *still in the Theatre of 13 Rows in Opole, playing the role of a local hero who led an uprising in Silesia. Then* The Idiot, *from Dostoevsky, directed by Krygier and played by the company.*

Molik: There I sang two arias from Tchaikovsky, one from *Onegin* and the other from *Dame de Pique*.

Campo: *How come Grotowski wasn't the director?*
Molik: It was just a distraction. He agreed with it.
Campo: *Then there was the cabaret.*
Molik: Yes the *Kabaret Błażeja Sartra*. It was cabaret. It was a kind of cabaret we did by ourselves, without Grotowski.
Campo: *And you were director there.*
Molik: Yes, I was directing it.
Campo: *So that year you had your first experiences as director.*
Molik: Yes, the first and the last.
Campo: *Actually, I know that there have been others later on.*
Molik: Yes, but much later.
Campo: *It would be interesting to know more about these early performances, like* Cain *based on Byron, for example. How was it done? You were using a sort of avant-garde style, something like that.*
Molik: Yes. We did a duel with torch lights. Of course everything at that time was a personal suggestion because Grotowski wasn't much interested in such small things.
Campo: *You said he organised everything in advance but you still had a lot of freedom. So what was this organisation about? About what, if not the acting?*
Molik: We had freedom, yes. Yet, he was responsible for the whole performance. For the costumes, for the general direction, for the lighting and so on.
Campo: *Did you use music?*
Molik: No, there was just a guitar for music.
Campo: *You always played the music live, you never used recorded music.*
Molik: Never, just live, for years.
Campo: *You said you were enjoying life, but here you were always at the centre of the stage, as protagonist. And even later you were fundamental to all the productions. I reckon from the way you did them that it wasn't just a job for you, or an early apprenticeship, but it was something rather more important in your life.*
Molik: Yes, and I was so tired, I was so exhausted because of acting, that after *Akropolis* I had to leave, if you remember. Because I was physically not in a position to perform any longer in such a difficult situation. So I went to Cracow just to recover a little bit. For a year and a half. And then I came back in 1965 because there was an invitation to go with *Akropolis* to an international festival in Paris that was very important for us.

125

The company was without me the first time it went to Paris. Then we went another time, in 1967.

Campo: *But I believe that the early productions are also quite important. For example, Sakuntala, based on Kalidasa.*

Molik: Yes, it was a very beautiful performance.

Campo: *I can imagine, from the pictures I've seen and other information that I've got. And not just beautiful but also very important, because I think it was one of the first times that an Indian text was put on stage in the West.*

Molik: Yes, and in this performance we could now present not bad acting.

Campo: *It was the first satisfactory work.*

Molik: It was the first in which we could really present good acting skill as an ensemble, and not just me, who was already an actor. In this show for the first time we presented the qualities also of Rena Mirecka, of Antoni Jahołkowski and of the others.

Campo: *And in* Mystery Bouffe?

Molik: *Mystery Bouffe* was still my role.

Campo: *So the real change was* Sakuntala.

Molik: Well, not really. Not yet.

Campo: *How was* Mystery Bouffe?

Molik: *Mystery Bouffe* was very funny. It was really a very funny play, based on Mayakovsky. Once we played for just one person. It was a young girl who was in the middle of an empty room, completely empty, and she was laughing so much. It was an unforgettable performance, because since it was for just one person and she was laughing so much, we didn't just play very well but we were improvising. We almost did something like commedia dell'arte. And it was so funny that she was rocking with laughter on her chair all the time.

Campo: *But were the performances usually done for a normal audience?*

Molik: No, not for a normal audience, just for seven, for eight, for nine spectators.

Campo: *Just a few.*

Molik: A few, a very few.

Campo: *And what is this* Faust *by Goethe, in Poznań, in 1960?*

Molik: I wasn't there. Grotowski did *Faust* by Goethe in Poznań. Ours was the *Faust* by Marlowe.

Campo: *Back to* Cain *based on Byron. It's a very strong text.*

Molik: It is a very beautiful play, and it was beautifully done. It was just like singing, playing. It wasn't just a text, but also singing and a sort of dancing. It was half singing as well, and playing the guitar.

Campo: *And* Forefathers' Eve?

Molik: *Dziady*. It was a big national drama by Mickiewicz.

Campo: *Romantic then.*

Molik: A Romantic play, yes.

Campo: *How was it? It was your first big national Romantic play. Then you played also Wyspiański, but that was the first, so for you it had to be different from the previous productions.*

Molik: Yes, it was a very serious play. But of course, not in a regular way. There was a long monologue there: 'along and who you divine my spirit grasp the meaning of the song, whose eye will see the radiance of the shining'. In the translation into English it sounds like that. So there's this monologue, a great monologue, very long, twenty minutes long, like in *Cain*, where I played Alpha and Omega.

Campo: *Why did you say it wasn't done in a regular way? What do you mean?*

Molik: Because the hero of *Dziady*, 'Forefathers' Eve', was dressed like a chaplain, with his typical ornaments, but instead of the cross he was carrying a broom on his shoulders.

Campo: *So it was like making fun of the clergy.*

Molik: It was a blasphemy, a big blasphemy. So there was a little scandal. The critics were scandalised.

Campo: *Why were you doing it?*

Molik: Because Grotowski had these kinds of ideas, the concept of apotheosis and derision, something that is very high pulled over something that is very low. That's why we did it this way.

Campo: *In the same year there were two documentaries:* Clay Pigeons *and* Tourists.

Molik: These were just very small things, done without me.

Campo: *Then in 1962 we have* Kordian*, and the change of the name of the company.*

Molik: Yes, before it was Theatre of 13 Rows, and then we changed to Teatr Laboratorium.

Campo: *Yes, from Theatre of 13 Rows to Teatr-Laboratorium of 13 Rows and then just Teatr Laboratorium. Was it somehow particularly important?*

Molik: I don't know. He decided to change it with Flaszen. From Theatre to Teatr Laboratorium.

Campo: *And was it a change for you, or just a continuation of the same work?*

Molik: No, the same work.

Campo: *What about* Kordian*?*

Molik: It was another national Romantic play, by Słowacki. It was set in a hospital for mentally ill people. With, and on, bunk beds. There are some pictures.

Campo: *How was your work?*

Molik: I was a doctor, as well as the pope.

Campo: *The pope?*

Molik: Yes, the pope. I was playing two roles; the pope and the chief of the hospital.

Campo: *How did you build your characters?*

Molik: Normally, as usual. I was a doctor first, and then when I played as pope, I was a pope. There wasn't an actual building because it was rather a presentation of the characters. There was nothing important to analyse and so they weren't complex roles. So I was just dressed in white and I had a stethoscope, this device doctors use to auscultate.

Campo: *And then Eugenio Barba came.*

Molik: Yes, later.

Campo: *In 1962, when you were already starting* Akropolis. *Did he come after a while or at the beginning of the work?*

Molik: At the beginning.

Campo: *Did he influence your work?*

Molik: No, at that time he was just a practitioner.

Campo: *Basically silent.*

Molik: Yes, he was just watching and learning. And preparing good spaghetti, Italian spaghetti with *fruits de mer* and so on. I remember that, yes.

Campo: *There are different versions of* Akropolis. *What are the differences?*

Molik: They were different because some roles changed. These roles changed because I had to leave the theatre for a while.

Campo: *That's why they changed. It was all because of you, because you left.*

Molik: Yes, because I left. So not because of me, but because of my absence. But just some roles changed, not many, just one or two, but secondary characters. They tried to find another actor for my role but it wasn't possible. So there was a break for a year and half and then, when I came back we reconstructed it.

Campo: *So it was almost the same.*

Molik: Yes, it was exactly the same. They tried to make a substitution, to replace my role with Cieślak, but it wasn't possible at all, and so they gave up. Grotowski gave up.

Campo: *So Cieślak was already ready to do a big job.*

Molik: Not yet, no. It was a fundamental work, but he actually started in *Faust*. Cynkutis played Faust but Cieślak was Benvolio, and that was already his big role. Because he started working with Grotowski personally and that was the first step. Later he was the Constant Prince. Cieślak appeared also in *Hamlet*. He did a fantastic role in *Hamlet*. In the bathroom, taking an imaginary shower, he did it in a genius manner. Just one scene but …

Campo: Akropolis *was a very particular work for you.*

Molik: For the first time we tried to compose the performance, not to play it following this or that convention, but to compose it. So it was a new challenge for us, to find a new expression, a new means of expression. There was very little normal speaking there, rather a sort of singing, half singing and half speaking, and the speaking was very rarely natural because just a few sentences were spoken in a natural way, since everything was totally composed. So the speaking was never natural, maybe there were only a few, a very few sentences spoken normally, and all the rest was like a *partitura*, like a musical score. Everything was expressed as if there were notes to follow, very specific notes, and this was new for us. I'm not saying that there wasn't something similar before. In *Sakuntala* in fact there was already a similar approach, but it was of a different kind. In *Sakuntala* there was a more natural way, while in *Akropolis* everything was composed in a very artificial manner. So it was a new experience for us, for all of us.

Campo: *It didn't come from improvisations. It was created after a specific idea.*

Molik: Yes, it was like trying to create a living composition of notes.

Campo: Sakuntala *was instead created from your own improvisation.*

Molik: Exactly, and it was more like singing, normal singing, while in *Akropolis* everything was created artificially.

Campo: *So it came from someone else, not from the actors.*

Molik: No, it came from the actors, but the actors had to invent artificial scores, not organic as they were in *Sakuntala*, but like some sort of Stockhausen's compositions or something like that.

Campo: *What about the make-up? In* Sakuntala *the make-up was very important, as we can see in some pictures.*

Molik: That's a funny story. It was invented by kids, the proposals for the costumes and the make-up came from kids. That's because Maszkowski, the man who was responsible for all the arrangements of *Sakuntala*, had led some painting classes in primary schools.

Campo: *Because he was a painter.*

Molik: Yes, he was a kind of painter. I have a portrait of Grotowski done by Maszkowski. It looks awful, but it's very special because it's not normal, not naturalistic but decomposed, and yet Grotowski recognised himself, that he was portrayed there. It's very special, it's like an icon, like these icons we have in some small churches in the eastern part of our country.

Campo: *Then in* Akropolis, *the make-up disappeared completely.*

Molik: Well, I wouldn't say completely. The fact is that the masks were made by ourselves, with our own faces. Each actor had invented his own mask, and the whole performance was played with these masks.

Campo: *Yes, this is a famous moment, the invention of these facial masks in* Akropolis, *these organic fixed expressions of the faces. There are still some misunderstandings about their creation. Maybe you could say something about the meaning of it and the way they were created.*

Molik: I might say that they were absolutely invented individually by each of us. Grotowski told us: 'you have to find your own mask', and everyone did. There are some pictures and you can see them.[2]

Campo: *Yes, they are famous. I always wondered how you could keep the expression of the mask for the whole time of the performance.*

Molik: It's a matter of habit, of getting used to it.

Campo: *So they became natural to you.*

Molik: Yes, they finally became natural. At first we had some problems, we had been forgetting about keeping the masks. But after a few weeks there was no problem any more, they were just like our other faces.

Campo: *Were they related to the characters, or to your own personal experience of life?*

Molik: They were created from our own personal experiences, not towards the characters of the piece, of the performance.

Campo: *So it was like finding your own inner self, or maybe another nature of yourself.*

Molik: Yes, how it would be in different circumstances, in particular how the face could be in a concentration camp. So everyone followed his own imagination, his own feelings.

Campo: *Was this process carried out just for the face or also for the posture and the movements?*

Molik: Also for the posture, for the face as well as the whole behaviour of these kinds of human beings. It was connected with a special way of walking, of moving and everything else.

Campo: *What was your particular role? When we see the video we notice that you're in a particularly prominent position. Although there are lots of actors and the stage is full, your presence is particularly strong. How did it happen?*

Molik: I was supposed to be a chief of a tribe, of an Israeli tribe. There were two parts in *Akropolis*, if you remember well: the first part was Israeli and the second was Greek, where I played Priam, the Trojan king. But anyway, it was all the time the same character playing different roles in this theatre of prisoners of the Nazi concentration camp. It was indeed like a theatre of prisoners, who organise different scenes, for example a marriage, when they go with these metal pipes. One of those [pipes] represented for them Rachel with her transparent veil. Rachel was the pipe, the shape of the silhouette, covered with a transparent veil, which was just plastic, a piece of plastic. And in this way they organised their own theatre, just before going into the oven, to be burnt.

Campo: *Then there is a moment when you use your hand in a special way and start a specific chant, a very special part.*

Molik: Sitting on the other people's arms.

Campo: *What was it exactly?*

Molik: It was an incantation that I had to invent by myself. It was a hymn that he sang when he tried to quarrel with God. He was sitting on the arms of the others, quarrelling with God, who was above, in heaven. He was turning all his words toward the sky, towards God. In the beginning it was just like a kind of talking, it was still done in a very composed way, but like speaking, and later it changed, becoming an incantation, and I chanted it.

Campo: *Was it your own creation or was there music, a melody or something else to follow?*

Molik: It was all my creation, everything except for the text. The text I say is the original by Wyspiański.

Campo: *Then, the year after, we have* The Tragical History of Doctor Faustus *by Marlowe, with Cynkutis playing the main role. What about this work?*

131

Molik: For me it was one of the most remarkable performances, because I wasn't in the performance, I was one of the public, and it made such a big impression on me, it really thrilled me. Very often I felt terrified, really, physically. There were some moments when I could smell the sulphur of the Inferno. I really smelled it, for example in the scene when Antoni Jahołkowski was on his back and Cynkutis was hanging on him with his head down. He kept his knees on the arms and his head was very low, just a few centimetres above the table, since the action was taking place on the table. And Rena Mirecka chanted in such a characteristic, scary manner, with the throat half closed, that it was really hard to take. You couldn't watch it normally; you were inside it instead. I was sitting with the public but I was so touched by this. Some of the scenes were too strong for me to sit and watch, and I believe the whole audience had the same feelings. Yes, not just me, I was just one of the public, but the rest of the public had to feel the same as me. It was absolutely extraordinary on the level of transforming the present time, changing the place, changing everything. We didn't feel like we were watching a performance, but watching something so unusual that it seemed to be unearthly, not on earth, something impossible, somewhere else, and you didn't know where.

Campo: *Like being on another planet, and your role was just sitting with the other spectators.*

Molik: Yes, I had just one or two sentences, in the very beginning, as a guest, because the spectators were guests, at the table, during a supper, since the action was taking place during the supper. Therefore there were these long tables. After that I wasn't involved, I just had two sentences in the beginning, speaking to Faust, saying something like: 'Why are you so, in such a state that ... ' and so on. I don't even remember exactly what I said, but I know that it was a question asked to Faust. And afterwards I was just sitting, and on the other side of the table there was Maciej Prus, who later became quite a well-known Polish director, but at that time was a very young actor, and we played these two guests. He was also saying one or two sentences, a few words. Later there was a terrible scene when Cieślak as Benvolio started the destruction of these tables. What he said physically was grave and incredible, on another level of reality. He started destroying all these tables and he stopped right before the spectators' noses. He took the tops of the tables completely apart, so it was a very, very difficult scene for him, not causing any harm to the people in the audience. He was in a state of madness, so everything was very violent, all his actions were very violent. However, all these actions must be incredibly precise, so as not to make any false movement and not to harm anyone. It could have ended as a tragedy for someone. So it was my preferred performance, of all the performances that I ever saw by our ensemble. Later I was taken very strongly into the action of the performance only in some exceptional but very few moments. Very few in *The Constant Prince*. While I felt this *Faust* very, very strongly for about half of the performances, of which there were about ninety. And I felt with the same intensity maybe just four, maybe five performances of *The Constant Prince*.

Campo: *The reason why you were playing just a guest in this Faust was that at that time you had a period in which you needed to be out of the company, to take a break and then go to a normal theatre in Cracow. What did you play there exactly?*

Molik: Nothing important, just some very popular, almost boulevard repertoire.

Campo: *More than one show?*

Molik: Yes, more. I'd been a year and a half in Cracow. At the time of *Faust* I was already exhausted. I was so physically tired that I couldn't go on any longer.

Campo: *You needed a break.*

Molik: Yes, it was the beginning of the break; in fact, later I went to Cracow to take a rest in the normal theatre, the Teatr Bagatela. I took my holiday for a year and a half there in Cracow. It was in 1964. I was there until the very end of the season in 1964.

Campo: *So you were living there. But before that time you were with the company, still working in the same way, with your training and all the rest. You weren't out of the situation, you were involved in everything. We have only a few fragments of* Faust *on video, but there we can see the great scene of Cynkutis playing with the wind.[3] It's quite clear that there was the practice of an exercise behind it, which is the opposition of vectors. Have you worked with it? I wonder if it's true that you were working at that time with these exercises of opposite vectors.*

Molik: Yes, we used to do all these physical and plastic exercises all the time.

Campo: *And what exactly is the work on opposite vectors?*

Molik: It's precisely that you work on opposite vectors, with the different directions and so on, opposite directions of actions.

Campo: It can be done with any movement.

Molik: Yes, of course.

Campo: Then we have the Study on Hamlet, *based on Wyspiański's version of the Shakespearian play. This is known as a big change for you; it seems that starting from here you developed a different approach to the work. In particular it was the moment when you started to move towards the concept, and the practice, of the Via Negativa.*[4]

Molik: We put aside any composition. So far there had always been some different kinds of composition in our performances. This time, with *Hamlet*, we took the first step toward this sort of research on the organism itself, leaving all composition aside.

Campo: *Then, from January 1964, there were other versions of* Akropolis. *You played* Akropolis *until 1967; the fifth and last version was performed in May of that year.*

Molik: We played it for so many years; it was probably the most-played of the performances we did. There are different versions just because, as I said, some minor roles changed. Szajna, who was a former actual prisoner of the concentration camp in Auschwitz, was the designer of the costumes and Gurawski the author of the set design and the composition of the space.

Campo: *In 1965 there were lots of things. That's the year of* The Constant Prince. *But before there were other things, like* The Dove, *a short film made in 1964 where you play with a dove. What was that? Why did you make it, what was the occasion?*

Molik: It was just a very short film made in a prison cell with a dove, with a pigeon. It was shot in Opole, for an amateur club, Kręciołek. There I'm imprisoned in a cell and a dove comes in. A young boy asked me to act in it, and I just did it. But it was nothing in particular, just a simple, amateur, very normal film, which won some prizes later on in a festival for amateur filmmakers. But it's very short.

Campo: *Short, yes, but let me say not very normal, I've seen it. I wondered about the end of the pigeon, because it seems to be treated very badly.*

Molik: Have you seen it? I haven't. Only once, but at the time, and never later. I don't remember what happened in this film. Anyway I've played a few roles in other films, but there's nothing interesting to say about it in this context.

Campo: *In the middle of the sixties you did* Etelme, *which is an actor-oratorium. What was it exactly?*

Molik: It was one of those events which take place occasionally. It was probably done on the occasion of the death of a man who was well known in Silesia. Silesia is a region of Poland, Śląsk in Polish. It was something like an *oratorium* [a eulogy], something done in memory of someone. It's a kind of montage, there are some poems, there are some *cantate*. Sometimes with a big orchestra, a big choir, as well as some recitations. If I remember well, at that time it was done with a symphony orchestra on the stage, and with three actors.

Campo: *In 1965 you played Robert in* Latajacych Narzeczonych, *in Cracow. What was it?*

Molik: It was *Boeing Boeing*. The title was *Boeing Boeing,* like the big airplane, or *The Flying Bride.* It was about a young woman who is going to get married. It was just a very popular play, just entertainment, pure entertainment. There was nothing of importance there.

Campo: *Then in 1966 Mówca in* Strachu i Nędzy Trzeciej Rzeszy *by Brecht. Do you remember what it was?*

Molik: Yes, I remember, it was just a kind of anti-war play, again at the Theatre Bagatela in Cracow; *The Fear and the Misery of the Third Reich* by Brecht, very political of course.

Campo: *How was it, playing Brecht? Did you use any special technique, any Brechtian technique?*

Molik: I have no idea. I don't remember what I did. It was of no meaning for me. Normal. It was still when I was in Cracow for my leave, my holiday.

Campo: *And the director?*

Molik: I don't remember who directed that.

Campo: *So it didn't have a strong influence on you.*

Molik: No.[5]

Campo: *I guess that you were already quite famous, so you were free to do whatever you wanted, or something like that.*

Molik: Yes. I just played my role. But I have no idea what I played in this performance.

Campo: *And then in 1966, in the same year, as a gangster in* Kiss Me, Kate, *by Cole Porter. So it was a musical.*

Molik: Yes, a musical.

Campo: *Was it interesting for you?*

Molik: Well, I enjoyed it. I invented so many things there that it was a big joy for me. It was just like playing, I completely relaxed.

Campo: Is it the only musical that you've done?

Molik: No, I also played something like a musical in Łódź, where I danced.

Campo: You've also done dancing.

Molik: Yes.

Campo: Then you did another thing, as narrator in Dallas, W samo Południe.

Molik: It was a small montage about Kennedy's assassination in Dallas, when he was shot. It was just a kind of montage on stage.

Campo: And why were you the narrator? There were no characters?

Molik: There were no characters there. It was just performed with a narrator and some musicians. Tomasz Stańko played the trumpet.

Campo: Stańko the jazzman.

Molik: Yes, the very famous jazzman. But at that time he was starting, he was a student, and in this piece we played together. I was the narrator and he played the trumpet. And another very famous musician, Ostaszewski, who already had years of experience, played the bass, and there was also a percussionist.

Campo: So the music was jazz.

Molik: Not really jazz, they just played as a trio, just like three people playing, but not necessarily jazz, they did a sort of musical illustration. It was a musical illustration of what I was telling.

Campo: Then you came back and there was The Constant Prince to do.

Molik: Yes. I entered *The Constant Prince*.

Campo: But before leaving you had already started with it at the beginning of the work.

Molik: Yes I started, but then I left before the premiere and I entered later.

Campo: In one of the first versions.

Molik: Yes, in the place of Maja Komorowska. She had played Tarudante before me.

Campo: What had happened? How was it that she left too?

Molik: She left because at that time she gave birth to her son.

Campo: What can you say about your work in The Constant Prince?

Molik: That I needed a period of time for myself, some weeks, and then we tried together, we rehearsed with everybody, with the full ensemble for a week, and then I was in the role. I created a different character, since I wasn't obliged to repeat the same score of the actor I replaced. I was just obliged to find a communal language with the partners. So I couldn't invent too many new situations, but I was free to find my own character.

Campo: *Then, on stage could you do some improvisations or did you have to play always within the same score?*

Molik: I had to keep the same score, but not exactly the same. The same situation but not exactly the same score. It wasn't like in *Akropolis*, that when someone wanted to replace someone else he was obliged to do the same actions, the same score. No, here I was free.

Campo: *You created this strange character with a black hat and the umbrella. You talked about it a few years ago at the theatre of the University of Rome and everybody was shocked. In fact scholars, critics, practitioners, students, all have a certain idea of* The Constant Prince, *taken from the famous film, and this revelation completely changed their perception of the piece. Then I found some colour pictures of the performance with you and your strange character and I showed them in an exhibition at Kent University, and people looked at them with special interest. How did it happen that you created such a character?*

Molik: Normally. I dropped in; I started working with the text and made my role using the umbrella and the hat.

Campo: *And this idea of a modern character, coming from another world, put in a fifteenth-century set, was accepted by Grotowski and the others.*

Molik: Yes, after two or three rehearsals.

Campo: *Was there a relation between the beginning of the work in which you were involved and what you did after the break? Was there a connection, or was it for you a totally different work?*

Molik: No, it was completely different because before I had only started the work, I wasn't in the premiere of *The Constant Prince*. I entered *The Constant Prince* when they had already been playing it for half a year or so. And it was already a big success, well known all over the world. Before this play we were just known locally and from one or two festivals, but this was like a bomb, in Paris. When I entered it all this had already happened, they had already been with *The Constant Prince* in Paris, first, and then in Sweden, I believe, and then also in Italy, in Spoleto. Later, when they came back, after a certain period of time, a few months or one year, I entered *The Constant Prince.*

Campo: *I've read some articles about your performance in Iran. What was the experience like in Iran, playing* The Constant Prince, *which is a classic Christian play?*

Molik: It was very good, it was just one or two years before the fall of the Shah Reza Pahlavi. We were very much favoured and hosted by his wife, Farah Diba.

Campo: *Then you played* Akropolis *again, also in Edinburgh, at the festival.*

Molik: Yes, afterwards, in 1968. We went to America too, with *The Constant Prince.*

Campo: *You were playing the two performances in the same period.*

Molik: Yes. In the same period we were doing the two. We even performed in Mexico, in Mexico City just before the Olympics. There we probably played *The Constant Prince*, or maybe it was still *Akropolis*, or maybe *Faust*. The Polish ambassador in Mexico City, a very nice and intelligent man, not like those who came later, had invited us. Later our ambassadors were different; he was one of those old-style people who came from the Polish Republika Ludowa, from folk people, from the people. I say people because *Ludowa* means People democracy, and in fact he belonged to that time of the People's Republic of Poland. And we had a big dinner, as you can see from the picture. There I recognise Flaszen, Rena Mirecka, Staszek Ścierski, Cynkutis, Grotowski and the chief manager Andre Sel, whom we used to call administrative director. It was a special dinner with a very special menu, with everything, with soups of all kinds, with all the *entrées*, with lots of desserts and all other kinds of courses; there were eleven, eleven lines of courses on the menu. Cynkutis kept the dinner menu among his papers, he kept it until his death. I saw it because his wife showed it to me. We also played in Munich later, during the Olympics when there was this attack on the team from Israel.

Campo: *I think performing* Akropolis *in Germany you might have provoked a strange sensation.*

Molik: In Munich we played something else. But we played *Akropolis* in Berlin, for example.

Campo: *It's interesting what you were saying about the change in Cieślak. He wasn't that ready at the beginning of* Akropolis. *He wasn't like the Cieślak we know from the other perform-*

ances, like Doctor Faustus *and* The Constant Prince, *where he is clearly ready for it. So, there was a quick development of his work in these two to three years.*

Molik: Exactly. It was like this, in these two years, even in one year.

Campo: *Then there is* Ewangelie, *1967. What is it exactly?*

Molik: *Ewangelie* was the first step towards *Apocalypsis cum figuris.* Actually the very first step was *Samuel Zborowski.* Then there was *Ewangelie*, and finally *Apocalypsis cum figuris.*

Campo: *Was it ever performed in public?*

Molik: No, that was just searching, and from that work of finding materials the final result was *Apocalypsis cum figuris.* *Ewangelie* was just research, like *Samuel Zborowski*, and they were never played. I wasn't present at that time. I came only when we started our research on *Apocalypsis cum figuris.*

Campo: *It's been written that* Apocalypsis cum figuris *was co-directed by Ryszard Cieślak.*

Molik: Really? I can't say anything about it. I'm not sure because maybe in the first stage of this research, when I wasn't present yet, something happened like he was a sort of assistant or something like this. But later no, he was just an actor, as far as I can remember.

Campo: *How was the direction of Grotowski in* Apocalypsis cum figuris? *It seems that it was something very special, something particular, that he used not to say much while you were working, not like before, really directing the actors. It was something different.*

Molik: Yes, because he knew nothing about it. He had the idea of it, but he had no idea of how to do it, while in the previous performances he always knew everything, all that he wanted to get, to achieve as director. But this time he didn't know. So it happened that he was waiting while we were trying to make some of the so-called improvisations, for example for two weeks, before making any intervention. We were working at night, from nine in the evening to five o'clock in the morning. We rehearsed and we tried to find material from the improvisations. So for example, he watched the improvisations for two weeks and we hadn't reached anything. Everyone was just trying, looking around with no ideas, and Grotowski was just sitting and nothing, nothing, nothing was coming out. But finally, later, it just happened that the big impulse came from Ryszard Cieślak. He did some crazy running all around the room.

Campo: How long was it?

Molik: Maybe just forty seconds.

Campo: And then what happened? Everybody found the Life?

Molik: Yes, that's why his role was very significant, very important for this performance. Then the Life moved on, and in two weeks the main idea of the outline of the performance now started to shape itself.

Campo: To create its own form.

Molik: Yes, but before that there was one month of nothing, nothing, nothing.

Campo: Why were you rehearsing at night?

Molik: I don't know. Because Grotowski wanted to rehearse at night.

Campo: For the first time.

Molik: Yes.

Campo: This is also the time when the idea of paratheatre appears. During the period of paratheatre you were still playing Apocalypsis.

Molik: Yes, when we finished the rehearsals for *Apocalypsis cum figuris*, we just had two weeks free and then we started already the paratheatrical projects.

Campo: How did the connection between the two things, Apocalypsis cum figuris and paratheatre, work?

Molik: That Grotowski finished with the theatre. We decided not do it any more. Grotowski decided never to do another performance in his life. We played *Apocalypsis* and then we did different projects.

Campo: Yes but Apocalypsis worked for years. And the projects of paratheatre were already started. During that time you were doing both works, the theatre performing Apocalypsis and the projects of paratheatre without performances. So I wonder what was the connection between Apocalypsis and paratheatre. I know that Apocalypsis was also used to contact people for the paratheatrical projects.

Molik: Yes, at the weekends we used to come from paratheatre, from Brzezinka and the countryside, to Wrocław. We were playing in our space during the weekends only, and then going back again to Brzezinka for paratheatre.

Campo: Wasn't Apocalypsis also used now to experiment with a different relationship with the spectators, a different kind of communication, different from any other performance? Were you now trying to create, or at least did something happen, *like a sort of closer communication with the spectators? Or was it like the other productions you did, with fixed scores repeated every time?*

Molik: No, it was similar, it was the same, it was a kind of show, it was a performance like the previous ones, like *The Constant Prince*, like *Faustus*. They were of the same kind, a similar type of performance.

Campo: *I know that many spectators used to stay for a long time in the empty room after the end of the performance. So it made a strange and strong impression on the spectators.*

Molik: It's true, at that time it was very strong for some people. It was a very personal experience for some people.

Campo: *After a while you started your own personal project. Voice and Body, in 1979, is the first individual project of this kind of which I've found tracks. Of course before there was also Acting Therapy, in the mid-seventies. What was the beginning of that?*

Molik: That of 1979 was just a workshop. I remember instead the very beginning of the work. I had no idea of what to do with a big group, since previously I'd always been busy with the voice, with the work on voice, but only with our group, with my colleagues. I'd done only once a very short workshop in Finland, at the theatre school, so I had no practice with people, of how to work with a big group. I started alone then, I just remember that it started in our modern room, in the smaller room, in the *parterre*, not in the big *salle* upstairs. Then one of the people just began a march around the room. And it started like this, first energy, and then singing, and later I slowly started to organise the work. I found the 'Body Alphabet', that the work had to be made not just out of spontaneous movements but out of more formalised and organised actions.

Campo: *So at that time, around the mid-seventies, you started composing the 'Body Alphabet'. How did the 'Body Alphabet' start? What was the process of creation of the 'Body Alphabet' like? Was it your own new research to create your own system, or was it like recalling your experience and trying to select some actions?*

Molik: To tell the truth I don't remember, but if I try to reconstruct it in my mind, to come back to that time, it must be that since I knew the actions of the *plastiques*, I took from them those that I knew could be useful, and I simply had to invent the rest. I had to invent everything. There was no precursor that I knew from whom I could take any experience. When I started, first I tried it with those of my colleagues who had problems with the voice, and then I tried with bigger groups from outside, with the people, and well, it just happened, step by step. The beginning was of this kind, practically without any knowledge, just doing something intuitively, and then working with fragments of someone else's knowledge, but just trying them out. I had to reject certain things immediately, I tried to explore more and follow certain other things, and everything always went like this, gradually proceeding with new elements.

Campo: *Anyway, each one of these, how to say, letters or actions, is always directed at opening the voice.*

Molik: Yes, this is the real goal, to wake up the connections in the body, to make the body alive and ready to give and respond to the impulses. The body must also be prepared for it, because otherwise you can only do some vocal exercises, and this is a quite different thing. I remember that in our theatre school we just did with this old – and on the other hand very good – person some simple vocal exercises, like singing the same sentence in different tunes, without the body, or just vocalising very simply something like 'oh-oh-oh-oh-oh', and that was all. My idea was different, so I started to create it.

Campo: *You created one exercise after the other, trying to find out what was good, and then all these formed a sequence, a precise sequence.*

Molik: They become a sequence, but not fixed. The way of joining them, the conjunctions between one and the other, is free.

Campo: *It can have a different montage.*

Molik: Yes, different, but you must know the actions off by heart, so that your body, without thinking, in a given moment, before ending one action, knows already what will be the next. So everything is fluent, the whole life is fluent all the time. Everything is fluent with full Life, for twenty, twenty-five minutes.

Campo: *Maybe some of the actions work for someone more than for someone else, or are they all essential for everyone?*

Molik: No, they're all essential for everyone. All the actions are essential, but once you've learnt them, you're free to use each of them at a different moment. First is the teaching, the body must know all these actions, later they're now free. Everyone is free to choose the action at any different given moment.

Campo: *Then the theatre closed, Poland was under martial law. Grotowski worked for a couple more years on the Theatre*

142

of Sources and then left, but in 1984 Cynkutis reopened the Institute in Wrocław, he founded the Second Studio. Did you collaborate with him at that time?

Molik: Yes, he became the director, he took the role of director, of chief manager, and I was in the group.

Campo: *In that period there are other things. A Project Studium in Berlin on Ibsen's* Peer Gynt *in 1982–83. How was your approach to it, what kind of work had you done?*

Molik: When I staged *Peer Gynt* in Hochschule der Künste in Berlin I did it so well that it was very much appreciated. I made seven people play Peer Gynt. That happened because there were seven actors, seven male pupils, seven students and eight girls. There was a role for each girl, but I had to put a different Peer Gynt in each scene, so all the male students played Peer Gynt. I did it in such a way that after every bigger scene, after certain specific parts, there was formed on stage a sort of pile of bodies and from this a new Peer Gynt was born, and so the next was another boy, and the same for the next, and so on. So there were seven, seven Peer Gynts in this *Peer Gynt*, and it was a very interesting and good performance.

Campo: *Did you create all this through improvisation, or was it your idea?*

Molik: It was my idea.

Campo: *So your work on direction was real direction, telling the actors what to do.*

Molik: Yes, of course.

Campo: *Then there is also a* Macbeth *under your direction.*

Molik: That was in Toronto, in 1985. I was invited to do a piece and I chose *Macbeth*. Of course I cut some parts, like the whole third act, so I made it last for an hour and a half only, instead of three hours.

Campo: *Was it done with students or professional actors?*

Molik: No it was done with all professionals. I had to do an audition, a casting, with hundreds of actors. I had to see them and make a selection.

Campo: *It was a production.*

Molik: It was an official theatre production, but the funny thing is that it was a *Macbeth* without Macbeth. The wife, Lady Macbeth was good, but the Macbeth himself completely lost his voice. He was so nervous that he had no voice at the premiere; he could just emit something like 'Ah … Iah … giah'. It was funny. However, there was an intelligent critic who wrote that even without Macbeth it was an interesting performance, with very unexpected, surprising situations and so on. But the others wrote that they wondered how they could watch a performance of *Macbeth* without Macbeth.

Campo: *Then there is* To Sing Or Not To Sing *in Berlin in 1987. This was again in Berlin but with another organisation, not the same as* Peer Gynt.

Molik: *Peer Gynt* was in Hochschule der Künste, in the theatre academy. This other one was a normal workshop for a group, which was finally organised as a show. I did a small show on that occasion. First I gave a ten-day workshop and then the organiser proposed that I do an official exhibition at the end. I remember that the cost of the ticket was 10 Deutsche Marks. The people came and what was presented to them was just what they had done in those ten days, and it happened that it was a good performance, interesting. It was just monologues and songs.

Campo: *Those that they had chosen for the workshop.*

Molik: Yes, organised by me.

Campo: *The last performance you directed is* King Lear *in 1990.*

Molik: Yes, I did it in the Wrocław theatre school.

Campo: *I guess with the students of the theatre school. How was it?*

Molik: Yes, I did it with the students and it was very, very interesting. There was a very good King Lear, a very talented young boy, who played it well. It was a good performance.

Campo: *Did you use any particular style or was it a classical approach?*

Molik: A classical approach, as far as the students go. But King Lear didn't act like a student. I can say he was already like a very spiritual actor. The others were just like students.

Campo: *You are an actor but you've had all these experiences as director over the years. What do you think of it, how is to be on the other side of the work?*

Molik: I had no problems with directing. I did it instinctively and from my experience, from my different experiences. I could organise the work, but I had no patience for all the perform-ance in terms of production. I just like the work with the actors; I never liked to be bothered with the lighting, the deco-rations, the settings and so on. That makes me bored. But I like very much the work with the actors. That's why I some-times accepted the proposals to direct, but these are rather episodes in my life because I never treated it seriously, I just took it as an adventure. Since I had the chance to be director, why not do it? I tried and it appeared that I could do it, quite simply. But they were never big events, as I said, I was just interested in the work with the actors, and that's not enough to be a good director, because a director must think of many more things, about and around them. Of how to create the sense, the direction of the sense, of what meaning he wants to convey through this or that performance. I just treated it professionally in terms of having to handle the actors, with the art of acting. And that's all. I was never deeply engaged in it.

Campo: *Did you work specifically on voice, with the actors?*

Molik: No, not on voice, when I direct I never stress this with the actors, I never put an emphasis on voice. These are two quite different domains.

Campo: *It seems that your directed works are very classical, like your-self if I may say, in terms of taste, poetics and style. But the avant-garde was very present at the very beginning of your work, also as an aesthetic approach. But you were probably never really engaged in the avant-garde.*

Molik: No, I just tried when I was in the theatre school in Warsaw. I took part in some experiments, in a few small projects of the avant-garde. But that was just a sort of game during my studies.

Campo: *In fact we can't say that* Mystery Bouffe *and* Sakuntala *were avant-garde.*

Molik: No, *Mystery Bouffe* and *Sakuntala* were not avant-garde.

145

10

NINTH DAY
Colleagues and collaborators

Campo: *I have a long, impressive list of colleagues and collaborators you worked with at the Teatr Laboratorium at different
periods of time. I wonder if and how they influenced your
work and life. Some are famous; we've already talked about
them several times in our conversations. For example: Ludwik
Flaszen. What was the influence of Flaszen in your work?*

Molik: I think that the role of Flaszen in our group is very important because it was him who got the offer to open the theatre
in Opole. And then he found Grotowski. But first there was
Flaszen, because he was very well known.

Campo: *He was already well known but he was still very young.*

Molik: Yes, but he was already very well known, and Grotowski was
not so well known.

Campo: *Why was he well known?*

Molik: Because he was already a famous critic, a literary critic who
used to write very good, interesting and witty *feuilletons*.
He was in Cracow. He was very well known in the whole
of Poland, but especially in Cracow. Then Grotowski was a
very young man, he was 26, just after completing his diploma.
He had no experience, he had tried to direct just one small
thing before, and that was all. But Flaszen saw potential in
Grotowski and offered him the post of director of this theatre
in Opole, saying: 'I will be the literary adviser'.

Campo: *How was it that he had such a power to open a theatre? The
institutions gave him the power to open a theatre, to pay sala-
ries I mean, just because he was already famous.*

Molik: Yes, the room and the financial means. The Opole authorities
gave the power to Flaszen to open the theatre.

Campo: *So they were the local authorities, not the national authority.*

Molik: Local authority, but it has enough authority, because there are no national theatres in Poland. There are only two, one in Warsaw and one in Cracow, and the rest are local.

Campo: *And how was his presence in all these years? We always talk of course about Grotowski, but Flaszen was there too.*

Molik: Yes, he was there, and he was very important because we can say that he was Grotowski's alter-ego. They used to discuss all day and all night what to do and how to do it, and he was also a kind of mentor for Grotowski.

Campo: *He was less present with the actors, with you and the others.*

Molik: He was almost not present at all. He had nothing to do with the actors.

Campo: *Rena Mirecka.*

Molik: She was from the very beginning a very original person. She was blonde and a *grande dame*. She was always very elegant. Sometimes she had nothing to eat because she was very poor then, at that time, but she was always very elegant and very chic. She was an inexperienced actress, but there was something that Grotowski found in her, and he suggested that she work with us.

Campo: *She went to drama school.*

Molik: Yes, she finished drama school in Cracow, like Cieślak. He also studied in Cracow, not exactly in the drama school, but however in something like the actors' school.

Campo: *What about her work, how was her presence over the years?*

Molik: She used to work hard, so anything she did was always OK. She responded very well to any suggestion by Grotowski, and Grotowski liked her very much.

Campo: *Was it easy for you to work with her, to work together?*

Molik: Yes, we worked together in the group and also in the cabaret, with Antoni Jahołkowski and one or two people from outside the company, and we did the cabaret for a while. We did it in order to gain a flat for Jahołkowski, because he was already married and he had no place in which to live in Opole. So we did it, and we invited the *burmistrz*, the mayor of the town. I was the *conférencier*, so I said a few words, saying what a genius he was and how good he was for the town, and then, after that, Jahołkowski got a flat. At that time an official person had such a power that he could give you an apartment, a flat to live in.

Campo: *Rena Mirecka created the* plastiques*, the plastic exercises or 'exercises plastiques'.*

Molik: Yes, she was the leader of the *plastiques*, of the plastic exercises.

147

Campo:	*You had to follow her when she was leading.*
Molik:	Yes, she was leading the lessons of plastics.
Campo:	*So practically, she influenced you.*
Molik:	Why not? We influenced each other, yes. With Cieślak it was different, because he was very demanding and he proposed very hard exercises. He was leader of gymnastics, of the so-called physical exercises, and some people had some problems with the knees, because he was physically very good himself and very demanding with the others.
Campo:	*Where did he learn these exercises, or did he just create them?*
Molik:	I don't know, but they were simple exercises, like gymnastics.
Campo:	*Antoni Jahołkowski. What about his work and his character?*
Molik:	He was a special man, very friendly, very open to everybody. He was very often a kind of homeostatic in our group, and very talented. He could play, perform, and also sing, very well; he had a very good ear, which is important in this kind of work. But above all he was a so-called exceptional person because he was so friendly to the others and to all the world.
Campo:	*Zbigniew Cynkutis. He was younger.*
Molik:	Yes, he was the youngest of all the actors of our group. He was known already because he had taken part in a film which was quite important in our history, in the history of Poland. And so he was already a little bit known before coming into the group, although he was still young; he came only a year after his studies. Yes, he was young, and he also died young.
Campo:	*He was also a strong presence in the performances, as an actor, as we can see in the photographs.*
Molik:	Yes, in *Faust*. And in the others, for example in *Kordian*, he was very brave, very courageous, he was never afraid of doing very risky things. I remember a scene in *Kordian* when he was saying the monologue on Mont Blanc, a very well-known monologue from *Kordian*. In our piece he was on the second level of the bed, so it was quite high, he was standing up, and from that position he was falling down quite stiff, because it was set in a hospital for crazy people, and he was just catatonic. And in this manner he was falling down on his back, keeping the body still and rigid. I was the doctor and at the very last moment I was catching him by the neck. He was never afraid, but he told me that he had so much trust in me that he couldn't do it with anybody else.

Campo: *Ryszard Cieślak. You've already said many things about Cieślak.*

Molik: Cieślak was completely inexperienced. He came just after finishing school and probably it wasn't a drama school, since he was interested in puppets. He finished at the puppetry department. He came and he had a big problem with sound, with voice, with his voice, because he was speaking all the time with the larynx half closed, so he had to work hard to open it. I've mentioned it already, that he laid on the floor for two weeks and for two, three hours a day was lying in such a position with only the nape of the neck and the feet on the floor, and the whole body up, to make sure that his larynx was open. And then he was vocalising this 'Ahhh', this famous, very low and half-closed voice that you can hear in an old film. He had this 'Ahhh' for a long time, but he managed to solve this problem alone, and later he just worked a little bit with Grotowski and he knew what vocal possibilities he had.

Campo: *But you worked with him, you changed his way.*

Molik: Not really, I just showed him what he had to do; that is, lying down and going up with the chest. But he did it by himself; he worked for a long time by himself. And later he made it more elastic, working with Grotowski, but then it was already open.

Campo: *He was a very strong personality and at a certain moment became a symbol. The Teatr Laboratorium became a symbol and he's still now probably the icon of the theatre of the last century, at least of the second part of the last century.*

Molik: Yes, that's true. In 1969 he was even given an award in the USA for being the best actor in the world.

Campo: *He had a quick development. In the beginning he wasn't that ready, he had to work a lot with himself and then, in a way, suddenly became something else.*

Molik: Yes, exactly, because he worked individually for three months with Grotowski, and Grotowski opened something in him. He was prepared physically very well, but he opened in Cieślak the secret sources of power, and then he became as he was.

Campo: *Do you mean for* The Constant Prince *or before? You said that he was starting before, with* Faustus*, where he already did something exceptional.*

Molik: No, with *The Constant Prince*, but with *Faustus* he was already extraordinary. That was also after the individual work with Grotowski. The way he jumped on the table was extraordinary. You know, I tried this jump on the table, and it was completely flat, and then he did it for two metres. When I tried it I did maybe twenty or ten centimetres.

Campo: *And you were also a sort of athlete at that time, you weren't a weak man.*

Molik: Yes, but not strong enough to do it like that. You must be exceptional. Grotowski passed to him the secret of how to do it. So he made a jump of more than one metre and half, maybe, from a flat position on the table. I tried it and I did it maybe for ten centimetres.

Campo: *So Grotowski and Cieślak worked alone also before* Faustus. *They did this individual work at that time.*

Molik: Starting from *Faustus*, not before.

Campo: *Stanisław Ścierski.*

Molik: I can't say too much about him because he was such a strange person and I was so normal that we hadn't much to do together. There were some couples in our group. I was always with Antoni Jahołkowski when we went somewhere in town, somewhere in New York or in Berlin or in London. Ścierski was always with Cieślak, they used to walk together, the two of them. The rest are not so many, because we were basically only five.

Campo: *Elizabeth Albahaca.*

Molik: A charming person, she still is. She's in Montreal now, living with Teo Spychalski, they're married and they have a kid and she's lecturing something at the University, so she's a big person now. But at first, when she came, she was like from Amazonia, directly imported from Amazonia. She came from Brasilia, I guess, so she was a very strange person. Nobody knew what language she was speaking, because sometimes she spoke Polish, but it wasn't really Polish. Sometimes she spoke Spanish, but it wasn't really Spanish. Sometimes she spoke Portuguese but it wasn't really Portuguese. However, she was a great person. A great person, and she married Teo Spychalski. Spychalski was our teacher for foreigners, for people from abroad. He used to teach them Polish and he used to do it in three months, in such a way that everyone could speak normally in Polish. I don't know how he managed it.

Campo: *Following the chronology, I can see a very long and complex story. In 1959 there is Barbara Barska.*

Molik: She was in for one or two years, then she left.

Campo: *I don't know anything about her.*

Molik: Neither do I. She was a very nice girl, but she couldn't assimilate herself with us. You must be a very special person to be able to assimilate yourself with the kind of rude people we were at that time. So after around one year she had to leave.

Campo: *Stanisław Szreniawski.*

Molik: The same, same story, as well as Tadeusz Bartkowiak. They came together and left together. Next?

Campo: *Ewa Lubowiecka.*

Molik: She stayed a little longer. She had played already in *The Idiot.* She played in *Mystery Bouffe* as well as Barbara Barska, but Ewa Lubowiecka played also in *Sakuntala,* as a deer. She was very solid, and seeing her as a deer was very special.

Campo: *You mean that she had a strong presence on stage.*

Molik: She was very solidly built.

Campo: *Physically.*

Molik: Yes, physically, and when she played a small deer, delicate, it was a very special contrast. She was a beautiful girl. She stayed in Opole. Now she's still in Opole, she's lived there all the time. She didn't change, she didn't come, she didn't move with us to Wrocław.

Campo: *Adam Kurczyna.*

Molik: Adam was a great poet, already very well known in Opole. He was already an actor at the same time, and he was at that small theatre there before us, before Flaszen got this small *salle.* So he was there, and stayed and played in some of the first pieces. He played in *Orpheus* based on Cocteau, and later in *Mystery Bouffe* and in some other pieces during the first years.

Campo: *Then he didn't follow the group.*

Molik: No, after one year, or a year and half, he went away from the group.

Campo: *Andrzej Bielski.*

Molik: He was very true and faithful to our group, even if he changed to the Teatr Współczesny in Wrocław. He came with us to Opole and later he changed to the Teatr Współczesny here in Wrocław. We stayed together for a long time, we were friends until the last moment of his life; he died around seven, eight years ago.

Campo: *Maja Komorowska.*

Molik: Maja Komorowska is Maja Komorowska. She is well known, a movie star and so on, and a very good teacher in the Academy of Warsaw. The students adore her, they like her very much. She's still very active and was very active during the hard times in Poland. She was actively connected to our cardinal in Warsaw. And during the hard time, during the state of war, she was distributing packages to poor people or to the wives or mothers of the men who were in prison.[1] She was very active in this domain. Besides this, she has been professor at the Academy of Theatre in Warsaw for many years.

Campo: *How was it for her working with you at that time? How was working together?*

Molik: We worked together and we even had special meetings, because she had problems with her vocal cords. She was chronically ill, and we had to work for one month to get it straight, to get rid of this disease.

Campo: *Maciej Prus.*

Molik: He is also now very well known, a very acknowledged director. He stayed with the group for maybe two or three years.

Campo: *Then, at the time of* Akropolis, *there is Andrzej Paluchie-wicz.*

Molik: He came to us from the pantomime. He was with us for around three or four years. He was a very good young man.

Campo: *Aleksander Kopezewski.*

Molik: This was a very short episode. He was a very, very special person. He was with us for a few months only.

Campo: *Why do you say that he was a very special person?*

Molik: Because his interests were quite different, and he found this kind of group just by pure accident.

Campo: *Mieczysław Janowski.*

Molik: He is still connected with us; he travels with us when there are some screenings of the film on *The Constant Prince*, because he's in this film. You know him, he's also a very special person, but in a very positive sense.

Campo: *Yes he is, he's also a friend. Would you like to say anything about the work?*

Molik: He hasn't been working as an actor for years now. At that time he was normal, it was a normal work and everything was OK.

Campo: *Gaston Kulig.*

Molik: He left, went to France and got lost somewhere in Paris. We haven't received any signs of life for years, because he left around twenty-five or even thirty years ago, so we don't know what happened to him.

Campo: *He worked with you just for a short time.*

Molik: A short time, a very short time, I think it was in the same period as Szreniawski, or maybe a bit later. He was with us for one year only; then I don't know what he did.

Campo: *Czeslaw Wojtala.*

Molik: He was good, a good boy, handsome. A quite handsome good boy. He was with us not for a long time; however, he functioned not badly somewhere later, in the domain of art. I don't remember exactly where and what he did, but I know that he proved that he's someone of value.

Campo: *Ewa Benesz.*

Molik: Normally she works with Rena. They made this kind of tandem lately, and she did a doctorate in Italy, so she's a very important person, now. She's a lecturer at a university somewhere.

Campo: *Was she an actress with you?*

Molik: She wasn't an actress but she was with us. She was in this group at Brzezinka, in paratheatre, and she specialised in paratheatre. She was never an actress.

Campo: *Teresa Nawrot.*

Molik: She was a rather strange person, I must say. She finally made herself professor of drama in Berlin. When she achieved the qualification of Master she created a private school in Berlin.

Campo: *Was she an actress with you?*

Molik: She was an actress, after acting school, but she never performed. She was in this paratheatre group.

Campo: *Irena Rycyk.*

Molik: She was also in paratheatre, at the same time.

Campo: *Jerzy Bogajewicz.*

Molik: The same, he was in paratheatre, not in the theatre. Now he's Jurek Bogajewicz and is a well-known director in Polish TV. He was in Los Angeles for a long period of time, working as a kind of director of cinema and of TV. He returned from the USA to Poland, and for the past two or three years he's been doing some programmes here on Polish TV.

Campo: *Teo Spychalski. Is he Zbigniew, the same person?*

Molik: Yes, he is the same; Teo is a nickname for Zbigniew. He's the one who has his own theatre in Montreal now.

Campo: *I remember him speaking in Pontedera. He was very interesting. What was his role in the group?*

Molik: He was a Polonist.

Campo: *A language expert.*

Molik: Yes, of Polish language, in Poznań. He came to us I don't know exactly in what capacity, whether as literary adviser, or a kind of archivist, or something like that, and he found himself very suited for paratheatre. He did very interesting things and later he got ready to have his own theatre in Montreal. Around ten or fifteen years ago he found an actor who was already well known there, Gabriel Arcand, they joined up and they opened the theatre.

Campo: *This is an example of those who started with paratheatre and then became people of theatre.*

Molik: Yes.

Campo: *Jacek Zmysłowski.*

Molik: Poor boy. He died in New York of an unknown and very mysterious disease. He was a wonderful person who played the guitar very well, played very well at tennis, who was very intelligent in his studies and so on. There weren't many of these kinds of people, of this class, in our group. Yes, he was a boy with class. But then, he died.

Campo: *He was also particularly crucial in building the paratheatrical activities.*

Molik: Paratheatre, yes. He had his own project, and in this domain of paratheatre he was very close to Grotowski. He did the project *Góra* at that time: Mountain.

Campo: *Zbigniew Kozłowski.*

Molik: He's one of those from the same period of time in paratheatre.

Campo: *Wiesław Hoszowski.*

Molik: He died a long time ago. He was also a member of this group from the younger generation. At a certain time, when he opened this project with paratheatre, Grotowski opened the theatre to the new generation, and he was one of this young generation. Like Alik.

Campo: *Aleksander Lidtke.*

Molik: Yes, Aleksander Lidtke. All the same generation, twenty, twenty-one years old.

Campo: *Włodzimierz Staniewski.*

Molik: No, this is another thing, Staniewski was here earlier, and he's had his own theatre in Lublin for many years now.

Campo: *Yes he created the renowned company Gardzienice, but after this experience. What was his work like?*

Molik: He was one of the leaders in this paratheatre.

Campo: *So he also started with paratheatre.*

Molik: Yes, as far as I know he was never an actor, he was selected for the new group of paratheatre and then he even worked with us in the Tree of People project. Maybe he performed sometimes, but not professionally, no, he was never an actor.

Campo: *I wonder how he developed all his system of training, direction and so on, since he never really worked with you in the company.*

Molik: It's true, he never worked with us in the company but he was a very independent and a very energetic person, so he quite simply found his own ways.

Campo: *Małgorzata Dziewulska.*

Molik: She was a kind of literary adviser, someone who writes about theatre.

Campo: *So she was following you and analysing your work.*

Molik: Something like that, occasionally also our work.

Campo: *André Gregory.*

Molik: He was from New York, a well-known actor and director who used to arrive here and also take part in the projects of para-theatre.

Campo: *Was he just a participant, or also part of the projects as guide or leader?*

Molik: A participant. I only know that he came here a few times, working not in the group of the young generation, but in a group of foreigners.

Campo: *Like Elizabeth Havard, Caroline Laney, Robert Weewing, Maro Shimada ... And later there were more in the two groups of the Theatre of Sources, with Jairo Cuesta, Abani Biswas, Magda Złotowska, and also Jean-Claude Tiga, Maud Robart, etc.*

Molik: Yes, they were in this other group I had nothing to do with, this is another story.

Campo: *Then I have those who then created the GIA, il Gruppo Inter-nazionale L'Avventura, in Italy. They were Fausto Pluchi-notta, François Kahn, François Liège, Stefano Vercelli, Laura Colombo and Pierre Guicheney.*

Molik: Yes, them. I remember Stefano, François and the others. I've met some of them sometimes when I've been in Pontedera, I've been there a few times. Last time I was in Pontedera was six years ago. Some of them were working there and they were doing good work. Here they didn't do much, but in Volterra and in Pontedera, yes.

Campo: *Well, I think that's all.*

Molik: That's good.

Campo: *I'm sure that it's not everything, but just a little part of what we can say. So, that's it.*

155

Molik: Good.

Campo: *I wonder if you want to say something else, anything, whatever you want, if you have an idea of the book, of how it should be done, or anything else, if you want to make any comment. It's your material, your work.*

Molik: It's your book and it's your responsibility, everything is yours.

Campo: *Yes but I make it to be yours.*

Molik: No, no, I just conceded something for this, to give you some material, but what you will do with that, is up to you.

Campo: OK.

APPENDIX: GROTOWSKI, THEATRE AND BEYOND

From Stanislavski to Grotowski – The Theatre of Productions (1959–69) – Paratheatre (1970–78) – Theatre of Sources (1979–82) and after

Jerzy Grotowski (Rzeszów, 1933–Pontedera, 1999) received his actor's diploma from the State Theatre School in Cracow in 1955. After being employed briefly at the local Stary Teatr he moved to Moscow to attend a directing course. His main teacher was Stanislavski's and Vakhtangov's disciple Yuri Zavadsky. Zavadsky was with Vakhtangov from 1916 or so until 1922.

In his book *Grotowski and his Laboratory*, Zbigniew Osiński writes:

Grotowski was enrolled in the G.I.T.I.S. [State Institute of Theater Arts in Moscow] directing program from August 23, 1955, until June 15, 1956. Under the supervision of Yuri Zavadsky, he directed *The Mother* by Jerzy Szaniawski at the theater institute. He was Zavadsky's assistant in the production of *Zialpotov* by L. G. Zotin, which opened on April 27, 1956 at the Mossoviet Theatre. His professors left him free to accomplish his routine apprenticeship. He met Zavadsky ten years later in the hall of Théâtre Sarah Bernhardt, where, during the season of Théâtre des Nations, the Mossoviet Theatre of Moscow performed Gogol under Zavadsky's direction. The old man looked at Grotowski, took his glasses off, recognised him and opened his arms to him. He also directed productions at the Mossoviet and Moscow Art Theatre, and he studied the techniques of Stanislavski, Vakhtangov, Meyerhold, and Tairov.

Jerzy Grotowski and Ludwik Flaszen, co-founder with actors Zygmunt Molik and Rena Mirecka of his company Theatre of Thirteen Rows in

Opole (then the Laboratory Theatre when it transferred to the larger town of Wrocław in 1964–65), were also highly influenced by Osterwa and Limanowski's Polish company the Reduta, from which they even took the logo, replacing the central 'R' with an 'L'. Stanislavski, and his approach to an actor's work on himself, in turn directly influenced Osterwa and Limanowski.

One of the clearest and most influential results of Grotowski's research was the continual modification of the spatial relations between actors and spectators, among the spectators, and between the actors themselves, done in collaboration with the architect Jerzy Gurawski, Grotowski's collaborator from 1960 onwards. This is represented by productions such as *Sakuntala*, *Dziady*, *Cain* and finally *Kordian*, set in a psychiatric hospital where the spectators were configured as patients, continuing with later pieces such as *The Tragical History of Doctor Faustus*, where the spectators were guests at Faustus' last supper.

Revolutionary concepts such as 'poor theatre', of the performer as a 'holy actor' revealing himself through the process of 'via negativa', and performance as a 'secular ritual' are made clear in the films and the pictures (published in Grotowski's key book, *Towards a Poor Theatre*) of famous productions such as *Akropolis* and *The Constant Prince*, the latter illustrating that icon of twentieth-century theatre, Ryszard Cieślak, at work.

Other pictures in the book and the film *Training at the Teatr Laboratorium* (quoted in the text) also show the actor training that has revolutionised theatre practice.

The productions
Orpheus *(1959): text by Jean Cocteau*

This first production was seen as a 'statement of intent' and was accompanied by a booklet-manifesto on the philosophy that inspired the new theatre, showing its readiness to enter into a dialectical relationship with the written text and all elements of the work.

Cain *(1960): text by George Gordon, Lord Byron*

Reviewing the play, Kudliński wrote that 'Philosophical dialogue turns into scorn, metaphysical shock into derision, demonism into circus, tragic dread into cabaret, lyricism into clowning and frivolity … there is caricature, parody, satire, vaudeville, an operating sketch, mime, a little ballet scene, and besides all that – an irreverent attitude towards the text … there are … an actor amongst the audience, actors addressing the public, actors improvising during some changes. A general tower of Babel and confusion of tongues.' According to Barba, the spectators themselves were designated as Cain's descendants, 'present but remote and difficult to approach'.

At that time Grotowski also directed a version of *Faust* by Goethe in a constructivist style for the Teatr Polski in Poznań, produced without his company, as one of the official duties given to him by various institutions to fulfil.

Mystery-Bouffe *(1960) after Mayakovsky*

This play matched Grotowski's inclinations, so on this occasion he did not manipulate the text in order to engage in a polemic with the author. Nevertheless, he combined it with Mayakovsky's *The Bath-House* and characters were freely shifted around between the two plays. He also included fragments of Polish medieval mystery plays and was influenced by both medieval drama and oriental theatre. The material comprised a few shields painted to represent individual roles, a tin tub, a black-painted bench and the theatre's minuscule stage, conventionally divided from the audience. The stage design was painted in the style of Hieronymus Bosch.

Shakuntala *(1960) after the drama by Kalidasa*

Grotowski staged this ancient Indian drama after having directed its first presentation on Polish Radio in 1958, making extensive cuts and inserting fragments from some Indian ritual sources. Seventeen years later, Flaszen said of it: 'We chose it because of Grotowski's weakness for India, without a doubt. In this play, we deal with the extreme mysteries: strange sounds and dances are made. The sense was that we were all naïve, child-like, vis-à-vis these mysteries. And so the costumes, for example, were actually made by children.' This play sees the beginning of the collaboration with Gurawski.

Dziady *(Forefathers' Eve) (1961): text by Adam Mickiewicz*

Dziady is the principal play of the Polish Romantic period. It concerns the revolt of an individual against prevailing conventions where, by the power of poetry, the protagonist's personal drama transforms itself into a national drama. Here Grotowski attempted a total integration of actors and spectators by treating them as participants, exposing the relationship between ritual and play. It was from a review of this show that Grotowski took the key phrase the 'dialectic of apotheosis and derision'. Grotowski described how he treated one of the main scenes in these terms: 'The long soliloquy has been changed into the Stations of the Cross. Gustaw-

Konrad moves among the spectators. On his back he carries a broom, as Christ carried a Cross ... Here the director used a specific dialectic: entertainment versus ritual, Christ versus Don Quixote.'

Kordian *(1962) after Juliusz Słowacki*

This is the second Romantic drama staged by Grotowski and his company. Kordian is a man who receives the revelation that he can find the ultimate truth by sacrificing himself for his country. Then he participates in a plot to assassinate the Tsar, but he is caught and sent to a mental asylum before being condemned to death. Grotowski chose to place the whole performance in the asylum scene, where the patient Kordian is administered to by doctors and is prey to his own delirium. The scenery was made using metal-framed hospital beds layered in twos or threes. The actors and spectators were spatially and dramaturgically totally integrated and had the role of patients imposed on them.

Akropolis *(1962): text by Wyspiański*

The poet set this play in Cracow's Royal Palace during the night of the Resurrection, when, according to a tradition, the classical and biblical characters of the old tapestries on the walls come to life. Grotowski transferred the action to Auschwitz, not far from the city of Cracow. The actors were the dead resurrected from the crematoria, the spectators the living. The costumes and design were made in collaboration with Jozef Szajna, an old friend of the Laboratory Theatre and a former prisoner of the camp from 1940 to 1945. This performance had five versions and was recognised internationally, touring abroad for many years. It has been considered one of the major theatrical achievements of the century, thanks also to the masterly interpretation by Zygmunt Molik, the company's leading actor, as well as those of the other members of the group. Here they demonstrated the highest possibilities of a formalistic elaboration in the theatre, expressed on all levels of the performance, both vocal and physical, such as the invention of 'facial masks'.

The Tragical History of Doctor Faustus *(1963): text by Christopher Marlowe*

Here the structure of the play was rearranged to show the final hours of Faustus' life before being called to eternal damnation. The scenic arrangement was made with a three-sided table, as in a monastic refectory, where the spectators and two actors were the invited guests to a sort of Last Supper. The atmosphere of the production was heavily religious as well as sacrilegious, and terrifying, the characters dressed in habits of different orders, with Faustus, played by Zbigniew Cynkutis, treated like a saint.

A Hamlet Study *(Studium O Hamlecie) (1964) from the texts of William Shakespeare and Stanisław Wyspiański*

The title was taken from an essay by Wyspiański analysing key scenes from Shakespeare's play. The Laboratory Theatre used extracts from both sources, presenting, according to Ludwik Flaszen, their own 'history of the Danish Prince: variations on selected Shakespearian themes. The study of a motif.' The motif was that of the 'outsider'. Hamlet was played by Zygmunt Molik and was associated with the image of a Jew, a choice that provoked disapproval and suspicions of anti-Semitism. The performance was an experimental collective piece of work, intended as an open rehearsal, and took place in a completely empty room. Although it was their only new work presented in 1964, there were only twenty performances to a total of about 630 spectators.

The Constant Prince *(1965): text by Calderón/Słowacki*

The text is based on Romantic writer Juliusz Słowacki's adaptation of the classic Calderón drama, as used many years before by Osterwa's company, the Reduta. It shows the martyrdom of Don Fernando, who was caught and became a prisoner of the Moors after a battle. He is starved and maltreated, but endures all this abuse with the utmost calm and resolve. They threaten him so that he might beg for his liberty in exchange for the now Christian city Cueta, where his knighthood was won, but to no avail. At last, Fernando's captivity ends, but only with his death, at a point when even his persecutors are shocked at his sufferings and touched by his constancy. This production marks a period of practical security for the Laboratory Theatre, with a transfer to the larger city of Wrocław and greater international public acclaim. Ryszard Cieślak's performance as Don Fernando has been seen as the summit of Grotowski's acting method and research, and the performer was awarded the best actor of the year in the United States.

The set was conceived as a sort of operating theatre where the spectators were cut off from the action, obliged to look down, taking the role almost of clinical observers.

In 1968 the first edition of the book *Towards a Poor Theatre* was published (based on interviews and public speeches, published in English and edited by Eugenio Barba, Grotowski's former assistant). It soon became a classic of theatre theory and practice which has influenced generations of practitioners worldwide, in numerous translations.

Apocalypsis cum figuris *(1969) based on texts from the Bible, Dostoevsky's* The Brothers Karamazov, *T. S. Eliot and Simone* Weil's *Prologue*

The Laboratory Theatre's last production had a long preparation period and its different variations accompanied the development of the company over a period of twelve years, during which time most energy was devoted to the investigation of post-theatrical forms. Initially the work was based on Słowacki's *Samuel Zborowski*, then on *The Gospels* (*Ewangelie* in Polish, which performance was shown in a few private presentations only). Finally, after three years the piece took the form that we know as *Apocalypsis cum figuris*, using fragments from different authors and a selection of the actors' suggestions that came out of improvisation, finding a particular contemporary significance in their approach to myth. Grotowski explained: 'In *Apocalypsis* we departed from literature. It was not a montage of texts. It was something we arrived at during rehearsals, through flashes of revelation, through improvisations. We had material for twenty hours in the end. Out of that we had to construct something that could have its own energy, like a stream. It was only then that we turned to the text, to speech.' The concept of 'poor theatre' was now extended to its limit and only the actors' actions and the spectators defined the playing area. The room was lit up with two spotlights and candles.

Paratheatre

After having undertaken a solitary journey to India, Grotowski reappeared physically transformed and with new ideas. Before he had looked like a typical podgy, 'existentialist' intellectual, classically dressed in black clothes, always wearing sunglasses. After this journey he became extremely thin, with long hair and a beard, wearing jeans and so on, like a typical hippy. In 1970, at the peak of his success, just as Jacques Copeau did in France in the first part of the twentieth century, Grotowski decided to abandon the stage and to move from what he called 'the Theatre of Productions' to new frontiers of post-theatrical research that he named 'Paratheatre', the 'Theatre of Participation' or 'Active Culture', involving in this challenge most of the members of the company, as well as recruiting new ones.

He began travelling and giving speeches in order to present the new developments of his research, while still presenting *Apocalypsis cum figuris*. This last performance was also used to attract participants for the post-theatrical activities, a kind of recruiting ground.

Holiday

The most important document about this phase of work was published in 1973 with the title of 'Holiday – the day that is holy', based partly on a shorthand record of Grotowski's conference at New York University, December 1970.

This is the crux of that text:

> Some words are dead, even though we are still using them. There are some which are dead not because they ought to be substituted by others, but because what they mean has died. This is so for many of us, at least. Among such words are: show, performance, theatre, spectator, etc. but what is necessary? What is alive? Adventure and meeting; not just any one; but that what we want to happen to us would happen, and then, that it would also happen to others among us. For this, what do we need? First of all, a place and our own kind; and then that our kind, whom we do not know, should come, too. So, what matters is that, in this, first I should not be alone, then – we should not be alone. But what does *our kind* mean? They are those who breathe the same air and – one might say – share our senses. What is possible together? Holiday.

Active culture

A few years later he explained:

> We noted that when we eliminated certain blocks and obstacles what remains is what is most elementary and most simple – what exists between human beings when they have a certain confidence between each other and when they look for an understanding that goes beyond the understanding of words ... Precisely at that point one does not perform any more ... One day we found it necessary to eliminate the notion of theatre (an actor in front of a spectator) and what remained was a notion of meeting – not a daily meeting and not a meeting that took place by chance ... This kind of meeting cannot be realised in one evening.

Grotowski attempted in practice to transcend the separation between performer and spectator, which he considered a practice of 'passive culture', through the organisation of communal rites and simple interactive exchanges between all those gathered for such events. This practice of breaking the traditional separation between performer and spectator took the title 'Active Culture', because there was no substantial difference, in terms of the nature of their activity, between the leaders – either experts or the new generation of recently added younger members – and the participants.

The projects

These projects were shaped in different ways and presented in the form of events, sometimes lasting for extended periods, attempting to provoke in the participants, who were no longer spectators, a deconditioning impulse. The discovery of a new relationship with nature was the first input for this research, which began in the forest near Wrocław. It was mainly based in the surrounding areas of the basic farmhouse at Brzezinka, before being partially transferred indoors.

Significant among these events were the Special Project, Acting Therapy (initially led by Zygmunt Molik), the General Laboratory (including nightly paratheatrical work sessions called Beehive), the Mountain Project (divided into Night Vigil, The Way and Mountain of Flame), Openings (Otwarcia), Vigils, Earth Project (divided into Vigil, Doing, Village), and Tree of People, where any division even between everyday domestic activities and post-theatrical work disappeared in practice.

The University of Research

From 14 June to 7 July 1975 Grotowski, with the collaboration of Eugenio Barba, hosted in Wrocław a session of the University of Research of the Theatre of Nations festival, which was intended to be the culmination of the whole process of work of the Laboratory Theatre, at last opened up to a wider public. This resulted in a massive event that involved numerous public meetings, presentations, performances, screenings, workshops and training demonstrations by the main protagonists of contemporary theatre from around the world. According to Leszek Kolankiewicz, during the festival there were at least 4,500 active participants in the various paratheatrical activities conducted by the Laboratory Theatre members.

The Theatre of Sources and after

Whilst the members of the company were carrying on their theatrical and paratheatrical work, individually and in groups, Grotowski developed new perspectives of post-theatrical research. In June 1978, during the International Theatre Institute symposium held in Warsaw on the occasion of the first International Theatre Meeting, he gave a talk mentioning for the first time the Theatre of Sources, a large-scale project that he was about to conceive.

He issued the following press statement:

> The participants of the *Theatre of Sources* are people from different continents, cultures and traditions. The *Theatre of Sources* is devoted to those activities that lead us back to the sources of life, to direct, primary perception, to an organic, spring-like experiencing of life, of existence, of presence. Primary, that is a radical, dramatic, phenomenon – it is an initial, codified theme. The *Theatre of Sources* is planned between the years 1978 and 1980 with intense activity in the summer periods and with a final realization in 1980.

In fact, this project absorbed Grotowski's interest over the coming several years, leading him to create different international groups and to take journeys in far countries and distant cultures, such as Haiti, India and Mexico – amongst other places.

In Wrocław, while other projects were still running, they hosted some protagonists from these encounters, such as numerous guests coming from Haiti, led by Jean-Claude Tiga of Saint Soleil, a group of Indian Bauls etc., as well as other international members of the group itself such as Abani Biswas and Jairo Cuesta.

The exile

In 1982 Poland was under martial law and Grotowski felt that both his work and his life were at risk. Seeking a safe place to settle, he moved to Rome, where he delivered a series of important lectures on his recent research at the University of Rome La Sapienza, before receiving an invitation from New York to teach at Columbia University for one year. Then he found support for a new programme of research at the University of Irvine in California. As well as a regular directing course, here he focused on basic physical techniques, actions and ritual songs that can impact similarly on any performer regardless of their belief or culture of origin. This course of work is known as 'Objective Drama'. He requested and obtained a special pavilion entirely made of wood to be built exclusively for this purpose.

Pontedera and 'Art as Vehicle'

After a few years spent in the USA, Grotowski decided to move to Italy in 1986, accepting the more modest offer of hospitality from a group of young but enthusiastic supporters of his work, who gave him the opportunity to conduct long-term research without the pressure of having to show any results until he was ready.

In the surroundings of the small industrial town of Pontedera in Tuscany, in a large building in the locality of Vallicelle, he established the 'Workcenter of Jerzy Grotowski' – later 'Workcenter of Jerzy Grotowski and Thomas Richards', with the addition of the name of his chosen pupil and heir. Here he focused on what Peter Brook called 'Art as Vehicle', working with young companions and pupils. The direct effect of this kind of work, the direction of all its efforts, was no longer 'horizontal', that is, delivered to spectators or to other participants looking for an exchange, as it was during Paratheatre and Theatre of Sources, but 'vertical', that is, exclusively effective for the performers themselves. Its visible result was the creation of *Downstairs Action* and *Action*, where there were doers instead of actors and witnesses instead of spectators. This has now had many showings in the presence of witnesses (who receive a sort of secondary effect, like witnesses of rituals) and explicitly constitutes a reconnection with Grotowski's first phase of work in the domain of the Theatre of Productions.

Jerzy Grotowski worked and lived in Pontedera until his death in January 1999. In accordance with his will, his ashes were scattered on the holy mountain of Arunachala in Madras.

PHOTOGRAPHS

1   As *recytacje*, 'conférencier' for the agency Aktors based in Cracow (Molik's archive)

2   As *recytacje*, 'conférencier' in the Polish Army ensemble (Molik's archive)

3   Saying goodbye at the drama school. Also included in the picture, the
Dean Prof. Kasimir Rudzki, his assistant Lapicki, Prof. Perzanowska, Prof.
Witkowski, Prof. Bardini, Prof. Sempolinski, and colleagues Zdzisio Szym-
borski, Wiskowska and Barbara Prosniewska (Molik's archive)

4　An early production in Cracow (Molik's archive)

5   *Gangsters* in Łódź at the Theatre 7.15 (Molik's archive)

6   In Łódź in a piece by the Hungarian writer Molnar (Molik's archive)

7   Playing at the Theatre Bagatella in Cracow in 1964 (Molik's archive)

8   As Fabian in *Twelfth Night* by William Shakespeare in Opole (Molik's archive)

9 In Opole as Maurycy in *L'été en Nohan*, the play about Frédèric Chopin's
   lover written by J. Iwaszkiewic and directed by Jerzy Ankczac, before realising his movie (Molik's archive)

10 Playing Brecht's *The Fear and the Misery of the Third Reich* at the Theatre Bagatella in Cracow in 1966 (Molik's archive)

11 Training at the Teatr Laboratorium (Courtesy of the Grotowski Institute)

Following: pictures from all Teatr Laboratorium productions directed by Jerzy Grotowski

12 *Orpheus* (1959) (Courtesy of the Grotowski Institute)

13 *Cain* (1960) (Photo by Mirosław Kopydłowski)

14 With Grotowski and the cast of *Mystery Bouffe* (1960) (Photo by Leonard Olejnik)

15 *Sakuntala* (1960) (Photo by Leonard Olejnik)

16   Forefathers' Eve (1961) (Photo by Ryszard Okoński)

17 With Grotowski in rehearsal for *Kordian* (1962) (Courtesy of the Grotowski
Institute)

18   Kordian (1962) (Courtesy of the Grotowski Institute)

19   In rehearsal for *Akropolis* (1962) (Courtesy of the Grotowski Institute)

20   With Rena Mirecka in *Akropolis* (1962) (Courtesy of the Grotowski Institute)

21   The Constant Prince (1968) (Courtesy of the Grotowski Institute)

22   Apocalypsis cum figuris (1979) (Photo by Lorenzo Capellini)

Beyond Theatre

23 The Teatr Laboratorium in Mexico City in 1970. Also included, the administrative director Andre Sel, Jerzy Grotowski, the Polish ambassador, Rena Mirecka, Ludwik Flaszen, Zbigniew Cynkutis, Stanisław Ścierski (Courtesy of the Grotowski Institute)

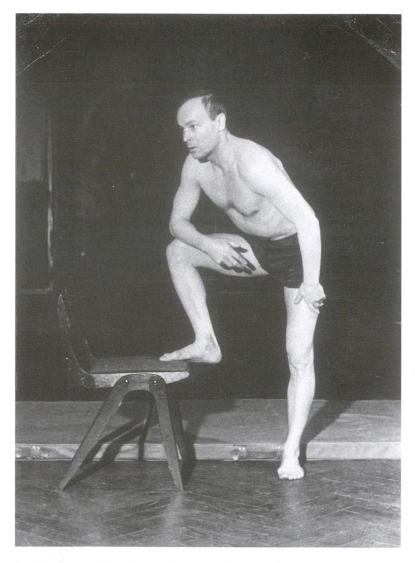

24   Early composition of the Body Alphabet (Courtesy of the Grotowski Institute)

25 In Brzezinka at the time of Paratheatre (Molik's archive)

26 In Montalcino (Italy) for a "Voice and Body" workshop (Molik's archive)

27 A work session in Rome with Ludwik Flaszen (Photo by Jan K. Fiolek)

28 With Katzu and Ioshita Ono in Paris in 1990 (Molik's archive)

29   At work in Wrocław (Molik's archive)

30   With Eugenio Barba during a session of the ISTA (International School of Theatre Anthropology) in Wrocław in 2005 (Photo by Francesco Galli)

31 Giuliano Campo with Ferdinando Taviani, Eugenio Barba and Mirella Schino in Holstebro in 2008 (Photo by Francesco Galli)

32 A recent session of Voice and Body in Wrocław (Photo by Francesco Galli)

33   Portrait by Francesco Galli, Wrocław 2008

NOTES

1 FIRST DAY

1 This article was temporarily available online and never published in print.
2 K. Stanislavski, *An Actor's Work: A Student's Diary*, edited and translated by Jean Benedetti, New York: Routledge, 2008.
3 *Akropolis*, play directed by Jerzy Grotowski; film director, James MacTaggart. GB: Arthur Cantor Films, 1968. Based on the play *Akropolis* by Stanisław Wyspiański. Preceded by Peter Brook's comments on the significance of Grotowski's setting.
4 *Theatre Laboratorium (List z Opolo, 'A Letter from Opole')*. Produced by P. W. S. Tif. Łódź, 1963. Diploma Film. Directed by Michael Elster. This is the first film of Grotowski's physical and vocal training from Opole, with fragments from the performance of *Faust*.

2 SECOND DAY

1 I have kept some of the French terms we used throughout our conversations in order to preserve the necessary amount of precision in their meaning. As a matter of fact, Molik's and Grotowski's second language was French and some of the technical terms they used were coined in French. (Author's note)
2 This film, produced and curated by Ferruccio Marotti and Luisa Tinti of the University of Rome 'La Sapienza' is not yet on the market.
3 J. Grotowski, *Towards a Poor Theatre*, London: Methuen, 1973.
4 A. Artaud, *The Theatre and Its Double*, New York: Grove Press, 1958.
5 Molik refers to the continental European pantomime, theatre made of gestures only. In English this is normally translated as 'mime'.
6 Theorist, director and founder of the company Odin Teatret based in Holstebro, Denmark, formerly Grotowski's assistant and editor.
7 In Rynek, now head office of the Grotowski Institute.
8 I have to clarify that Molik's idea of tradition relates to research of the sources of each human being rather than the theatrical roots. In fact he created his own techniques and never referred to any other method, whilst still claiming to belong to the tradition. This is indeed the specific approach revealed by the operation of maieutics as an exploration of the self. (Author's note)

3 THIRD DAY

1   For basic information about Paratheatre see the Appendix. For a more extensive understanding of the phenomenon, see J. Kumiega, *The Theatre of Grotowski*, London: Methuen, 1985.
2   This group was created by some international people who worked in Poland for a while and who then developed their own autonomous paratheatrical work in Italy, in Volterra in Tuscany. This was the only independent paratheatre group, although still connected with Grotowski. Their leader was the Sicilian Fausto Pluchinotta.
3   See T. Richards, *The Edge-Point of Performance*, Pontedera: Documentation Series of the Workcenter of Jerzy Grotowski, 1995.
4   See Appendix.
5   Italian scholar, Professor of History of Theatre at the University of L'Aquila.
6   See J. Grotowski, *Towards a Poor Theatre*, London: Methuen, 1973.

5 FIFTH DAY

1   Former member of Teatr Laboratorium.
2   Former member of the company and director of the Second Studio, opened in Wrocław in 1984 after Grotowski left the country.
3   *Training at the Teatr Laboratorium in Wrocław*, directed by Torgeir Wethal, produced by Odin Teatret Film, 1972.

7 SIXTH DAY

1   French actor (Crozon, 1887–Paris, 1951) who was considered the greatest of his time. He had a stammering and diction problem as a youth.
2   See Appendix.

8 SEVENTH DAY

1   French philosopher (Paris, 1909–Ashford, 1943).
2   See J. Grotowski, 'Performer', in Richard Schechner and Lisa Wolford (eds), *The Grotowski Sourcebook*, London, New York: Routledge, 1997, pp. 374–8.
3   Towards the end of *Apocalypsis cum figuris*, in the candlelit sequence, just before he is driven out by the Simpleton (Ryszard Cieślak) as the last of the money-changers in the temple, John (Stanisław Ścierski) makes the following profession to him in this speech adapted from Simone Weil's 'Prologue': 'You came into my room and said: "Poor is he who understands nothing who knows nothing. Come with me and I will teach you things you never dreamed of". You told me to leave and go with you to the attic, where from the open window one could see the entire city, a sort of wooden scaffolding and a river on which boats were being unloaded. We were alone. From a cupboard you took bread which we shared. The bread truly had the taste of bread. Never again did I perceive such a taste. You promised to teach me but you taught me nothing. One day you told me: "and now go". I never tried to find you again. I understood you came to me by mistake. My place is not in that attic. Anywhere else: in the prison cell, a railroad

waiting room, anywhere but not in that attic. Sometimes I can't keep from repeating, with fear and a remorseful conscience a little of what you told me. But how can I convince myself that I remember? You won't tell me, you are not here. I well know that you don't love me. How could you have loved me? And yet, there is within me something, a small part of me which, in the depths of my soul, trembling with fear, can't defend itself against the thought that maybe, in spite of everything, you ... Oh, Jesus!' [From the original programme in English of *Apocalypsis cum figuris*.]

9 EIGHTH DAY

1   See the photo gallery in the accompanying DVD.
2   See J. Grotowski, *Towards a Poor Theatre*, London: Methuen, 1973.
3   In *Theatre Laboratorium (List z Opolo, 'A Letter from Opole')*. Produced by P. W. S. Tif. Lódz, 1963. Diploma Film. Directed by Michael Elster.
4   Grotowski gradually elaborated this revolutionary approach to the work with actors, based on subtraction rather than on the addition of elements, as described in his *Towards a Poor Theatre*.
5   It is important to note that this information recalls a time when Poland was a socialist country, a place where actors were paid by official branches of the government, and quite often for the purposes of propaganda; it shows that Molik never followed Brecht's techniques with a specific interest and they were consequently never crucial to his work; that for him all the acting work he did outside of Grotowski's company was forgettable, which reinforces the impression of the uniqueness of the experience with Grotowski, something that he remembers in great detail. (Author's note)

10 NINTH DAY

1   Molik refers here to the time of martial war and the *coup d'état* of 1981, when a 'state of war' was declared in Poland.